P9-EFI-360

Growing Daylilies

Growing Daylilies

Graeme Grosvenor

Kangaroo Press

Cover: 'Entrancette' bred in Australia by
Barry Blyth (*Photo:* Barry Blyth). This is a
prolific flowering dormant tetraploid. The colour
is plum wine with a gold heart. A feature of it is
that it opens many blooms simultaneously.

© Graeme Grosvenor 1986

Reprinted 1990
First published in 1986 by Kangaroo Press Pty Ltd
3 Whitehall Road (P.O. Box 75) Kenthurst NSW 2156
Printed in Hong Kong by Colorcraft Ltd

ISBN 0 86417 084 X

CONTENTS

INTRODUCTION

The hemerocallis or daylily is an ancient plant known before written language. It probably originated in China although species have been found in Japan. The daylily was known to the Greeks in early Christian times and it is from the Greek *hemero* — one day, *callis* — beauty that Linnaeus in 1753 named the genus *Hemerocallis*.

Daylily! What a misnomer. It is not a lily, although a member of the lily family, and the 'day' tag is also rather misleading. Each flower does last only one day but a well established clump of hemerocallis will flower for up to seven or eight months on scapes which often produce in excess of 50 flowers.

Unfortunately many people identify the hemerocallis with the yellow species, *H. flava* or an early hybrid, seen growing wild along the roadside. It has been despised because of its toughness and ease of growth and it is only in recent years that the daylily family has gone though a resurgence of interest in Australia and New Zealand. Again we must pay tribute to the Americans who have taken a very ordinary plant and developed it beyond the realms of the imagination. From the original yellows and oranges we now have a full colour range of beautiful pastel creams, yellows, shades of pink and blends of these colours. There are rich vivid reds and purples, mauve, burgundy and violet. Some cultivars are bicolours while others have coloured edges or borders to contrast with or complement the basic colour. Many have fancy coloured eyes and different coloured throats. There is something for every taste but, as yet, no true blue or pure white. A real white is just around the corner but a real blue is still a hybridiser's dream.

Daylilies can be grown throughout Australia and New Zealand. They are frost hardy plants which will tolerate snow in winter while also thriving in the hot humid tropical northern areas. In general the dormant or deciduous cultivars do better in colder areas while the evergreen cultivars are better in tropical areas. Some evergreens are almost continuous flowering in the warmer parts of Queensland.

Daylilies are fibrous rooted, herbaceous perennials. The roots are elongated and finger-like, varying from thin and thread-like to large, elongated, fleshy and tuberous. Where the roots meet the foliage is called the crown and it is from the crown that the scapes holding the blooms emerge. The foliage can be dormant — the leaves die down in the colder months only to reappear in spring; evergreen — the leaves remain throughout the year; or semi-evergreen — the foliage dies back to a few centimetres in the winter only to grow back to normal height in the spring.

The daylily is a very adaptable plant and cultivars will often grow quite well in a full range of climatic conditions. We are very fortunate here in Dural in coastal New South Wales to be able to grow them all. It is never too cold for the evergreens and never too hot for the dormants. From a marketing point of view the evergreens seem to be more popular but the dormant cultivars will always be the favourites of the writer in our semi cold area. We rarely maintain good bloom after mid May although many of the strong evergreens continue to throw up scapes throughout the winter. 'Bishops Crest' seems to want to flower throughout the year. I find the new foliage of the dormant cultivars absolutely fascinating in spring. Each plant is distinctly different with varying shades of green, different shaped leaves and different veining in the new foliage. I find the new foliage every bit as attractive as that of the lovely hostas. Of course the dormant cultivars clean up their own clumps as they die down in autumn, altogether giving a much neater, more attractive plant. I can put up with the blank spot in winter while awaiting the *reverdie*.

Growing hemerocallis is a fascinating and rewarding hobby. Being an easy care plant a daylily can find its way into any garden no matter how small or congested, but the real enthusiast is the one who grows a full range collection and can still find room for one more. Because they are so adaptable, daylilies can be grown together with most plants and they often form a second hobby for those with a first love. Be warned, a second love can take over and become a first love.

Daylilies are ideal perennials for camellia and azalea enthusiasts. They can be used in the foreground and will bloom virtually continuously from the time of last spring blooms of the reticulata camellias and late flowering azaleas until the early sasanquas and reblooming azaleas start to flower in autumn.

Daylilies are also ideal perennials for orchid enthusiasts, again because they start blooming in the late spring when the main orchid flourish has finished and then provide continuous bloom until the orchids are again in flower. In tropical and warm temperature climates the seasons would overlap.

It is, however, with iris enthusiasts that daylilies have found most favour in recent times, and in the United States both the iris and daylily societies have large memberships. They are indeed the two most popular perennials grown in that country. While there is a flourishing iris society in both Australia and New Zealand a hemerocallis society did not become a reality until 1986. Mainly through the efforts of Margaret Lee, iris and daylily enthusiast of Arcadia, NSW, a daylily society with an initial membership of 33 — eight from Queensland, sixteen from New South Wales, four from Victoria, three from South Australia, one each from Western Australia and New Zealand — has been established. Mrs Lee has been installed as president and the first *Australian Daylily Journal* was published in February 1986 with Helen Reid as editor.

Why do the iris and daylily families go hand in hand and why do so many enthusiasts grow both? This is really a difficult question to answer although continuity of bloom is an important factor: the early daylilies come into bloom with the Japanese iris which finish the main iris season. However I would like to think that it is an appreciation of colour and form which attracts people to these two families of plants. There is an immense range of cultivars available which it is easy to add to by indulging in a hybridising campaign of one's own. Both the iris and daylily pollinate readily and produce hardy seedlings which give a quick return for labour as they bloom in two years from pollination.

By far the best reason for the joint growing of iris and daylilies is their respective ease of cultivation. Both are undemanding and rewarding families of plants which increase quickly and produce a lot of bloom in a small space and here the average daylily will far surpass the iris. Indeed for productivity over a period of time a daylily plant can only be matched by a rose bush and the care and attention needed to produce quality and quantity of rose blooms far exceeds that needed for a daylily.

Roses and daylilies can be grown together as good rose growing conditions are ideal for daylilies. They flower simultaneously for most of the year, both producing flowers from late spring through into late autumn or early winter. While I have never found a totally satisfactory companion plant for roses which, in my view, need to be grown alone in an open uncluttered position for the best results, a large bed of daylilies kept together with, but separate from, a formal rose garden is a beautiful complement to the roses if one has the space.

In thinking about growing daylilies in conjunction with other plants one must always be careful to keep the daylily clumps well away from the roots of plants which cannot compete. Beautiful effects can be obtained with careful planning, but a daylily planted between two roses 1.5 m apart would quickly rob them of their share of nutriment, as would also be the case with camellias, azaleas, iris and most other plants. The daylily is a tough customer and consideration must be given to the needs of other associated plants rather than to the daylily itself. If this is done, daylilies can be grown with most other plants because they will adapt to the conditions required.

One final word about growing daylilies with or near large trees or shrubs. Daylilies are highly competitive and will survive even if grown right among the roots, but survival is one thing and thriving is another. Underplanting ornamental trees or shrubs with daylilies is an excellent idea, but care should be taken to keep both the daylilies and their companions sufficiently apart to ensure that both get the nutriment necessary for good growth so that a pleasing effect is achieved. The choice of such trees and shrubs is really a personal one and most gardeners will choose their trees and shrubs first then come to the question of underplanting. It is only the occasional enthusiast who is going to plan a garden around a perennial, so it is sufficient to say that daylilies will cohabit with any other plants of your choice.

The daylily is an ideal plant for the lazy or inexperienced gardener, for the lover of colour and form who would like to be a gardener, or rather, would like to have a nice garden, but never can find the time or make the effort. It is a unique plant in that it forgives all the neglect heaped upon it and rewards its owner with beauty unsurpassed over an extended bloom season.

Daylilies are beautiful, easy to grow anywhere, tolerant of all types of soil conditions and garden positions and relatively free of pests and diseases. Cultivars are dormant or evergreen, range in height of scape from 20 cm to over 2 m, and come in a full colour range with flower size from 5 cm to over 20 cm in diameter. They also come in a fascinating range of bloom forms, are ideal in the garden or as cut flowers, and if you don't like them after all of that you can eat them. Yes, eat them! The daylily is an excellent gourmet vegetable and has been used for centuries by the Chinese in their cooking. All parts of the daylily are edible, so it offers the final challenge of being by far the most attractive vegetable in the garden or alternatively the most practical of flowering ornamentals.

1. CULTIVATION

Position

Daylilies are very tough perennials that will survive under conditions that would certainly see an end to most other plants. They will survive droughts and floods. They grow in very hot and very cold climates. They grow in mountainous country and in flat coastal or inland regions. They seem not to be particular about soil conditions. They will grow in dry, well drained positions or in wet boggy conditions. They will grow in shade or in full sun.

Has there ever been such an adaptable plant?

Adaptability is one thing but optimum performance is another. For the best flowers daylilies require several hours of sunlight in a position away from the competition of the roots of large trees or shrubs. They will compete but why give them anything but the best conditions? Particular cultivars require different conditions for optimum performance and this learning about your daylilies is part of the fun of growing them. Some require full sun to bring out their best colour and absolutely revel in the hottest of summer days, while others will bleach and grease in the hot sun but be most beautiful in a semi-shaded position.

For best results give your daylilies a well prepared position with good drainage. They will repay you handsomely for your consideration.

If a plant does not do well in a particular position don't be frightened to move it. Some of the rich dark coloured flowers do 'grease' in the hot sun and may be more spectacular in a protected semi-shaded position, particularly if grown in very hot areas. In general, the lighter coloured flowers will take the hot sun better than the dark reds and purples. Hybridisers have worked hard on sunfastness and most recent releases are very well equipped to handle all but the hottest of hot days.

Ground Preparation and Planting

Daylilies are undemanding as regards soil and will grow very well in slightly acid or alkaline conditions, a pH range of $6 < pH < 8$ will give good results.

A good soil mix is 1/3 good quality garden loam, 1/3 peat moss and 1/3 compost or very well rotted cow manure. This mix is also very suitable for pot culture and daylilies are excellent as potted plants.

The soil should be worked to a depth of 15-30 cm (6-12") and will benefit from the addition of a fertiliser such as superphosphate or blood and bone or a 5:10:10 complete fertiliser.

Plant by digging a hole and making a small mound in the middle. Place the crown of the plant on this mound and spread the roots

9

evenly. The plant will benefit from the addition of a tablespoon of 8-9 month slow release fertiliser such as Osmocote or Nutricote at planting time. Care must be taken to ensure that the crown of the plant is not less than 2.5 cm (1") or more than 5 cm (2") below the surface of the soil. Planting too deep will result in lack of bloom and poor increase. Cover with soil and dish inwards to ensure water gets to the roots. Firm the plants in solidly, using your feet if necessary.

While daylilies can be planted throughout the year in all but the coldest climates I have found that late autumn and early spring are the best times for establishing new plants. Plants set out in April or May establish new roots quickly while there is good warmth in the soil and they are well entrenched before winter cold sets in. There is no reason to cease planting during the winter months although plants will take longer to establish, but some nurserymen do not like handling the dormant plants at this time of the year.

When the soil starts to warm up in late August we come to another excellent planting time as plants again establish very quickly and with good after care will flower in early summer of the same season. September and October are therefore good planting months.

Here in Dural we get our first flowers in mid to late November thus following on the end of the tall bearded and Louisiana iris seasons and this initial bloom continues until after Christmas and often into the new year. Repeat bloom and continuous bloom on some cultivars then ensures flowers right through till June. There is no other perennial that will provide anything like the bloom of an established clump of a continuous blooming daylily.

When planting direct from one garden to another the gardener is in control of the time of moving and can avoid adverse weather conditions, but mail order plants have a habit of arriving at the most inconvenient times. If newly acquired plants arrive dry or at a time inconvenient for planting they should be soaked in water for anything from a few hours to a few days. Let them stand with the roots and crown immersed in water and if they must wait for a week or more a light covering of sand and a shady position outdoors will ensure top condition.

If you are purchasing from a reputable nurseryman, your plants will arrive with foliage and roots trimmed. Before planting give the plants a wash and remove any roots damaged in digging or transportation. This little extra care will ensure a healthy clean plant gets a good start in its new position.

The spacing of your daylilies is really a question of personal taste just as the positioning of different colours and patterns in a mass planting should be done to give pleasure to the gardener. Most daylilies are robust growers and quick increasers and it is advisable to leave 60-70 cm on each side of a plant to allow for future growth. Some gardeners like the massed effect and 60-70 cm distancing will give this in a season. Others like to see established clumps grown for the beauty of the individual clump and planting 1 m apart is really necessary unless clumps are going to be dug and replanted quite often.

Replanting

As already stated clumps should be lifted and divided after 3-4 years in the same position. The timing of this replanting is not critical and a lot depends on (1) the cultivar and its period of bloom (2) the climate (3) the availability of time and ground.

In a temperate climate such as we experience in Dural I find the months of May and August best for division and replanting with the in-between months of June and July quite satisfactory. In hot tropical climates I would think mid winter a better choice, while in colder climates April/May or September/October would be best.

Established clumps have their roots very well set into the ground and they should be gradually loosened with a heavy garden fork by working in rotation around the clump until it is free. A fork is much better than a spade for digging daylilies as its use will result in minimal damage to the roots.

Once lifted from the ground the clump can have the soil loosened from its roots with a few prodigious thumps onto something solid and then washed clear with a hose. The clump is then ready for division and a good sharp carving knife is excellent fo the initial cutting. I like to cut a clump up initially into three or four smaller clumps and then proceed to work on the smaller clumps which are usually easily broken up by hand. Take care not to divide the clump too hard as very small plants are

Lift clump with a fork

Cut clump into a number of sections using a sharp knife

Break sections into smaller divisions consisting of one, two, or three fans

Plant divisions

Dividing a clump of daylilies

often difficult to re-establish. For re-planting I would suggest two or three crowns maintained together will give the best start. When sending out plants from the nursery we always send double divisions, where stock allows, to ensure the customer gets a good start.

Some gardeners have that rare ability to enjoy their plants without having to have names or labels but, apart from the commercial impracticability of not doing so, I am afraid that I must have my precious plants labelled. After years of trying one system after another I have settled on old venetian blinds cut up and written on with a soft (6B) pencil or inscribed with dymo lettering. Just where the compromise between clear and legible labelling and obtrusive interference with the beauty of the plant lies I leave to the judgement of the gardener, but one important suggestion I do make is to have a written planting guide as a back up. This will eventually defeat the unwelcome attention of children, animals and, in our case particularly, currawongs, all of which seem to have an unmitigated desire to rearrange any labelling plan the author devises.

An excellent range of plastic labels is now available commercially and many would find their ease of handling and uniformity desirable.

After Care and Future Care

Once planted, a daylily is best left in the ground for a period of three years. Some cultivars are very vigorous and may need dividing earlier, while others that are slower growers could possibly be left for a fourth year. If the clump becomes overcrowded, division and replanting is essential as flowers on undivided clumps get smaller and fewer with the years. One well known American grower recommends dividing every year and insists that flowers on first year clumps are larger and better. It is my experience that this is true of some very vigorous cultivars and the autumn bloom on many newly planted varieties is superb, but, in general, the best flowers and the best scapes are on second and third year clumps.

To obtain these quality flowers on quality scapes we must look to the after care of a new plant. Once the new plant is established and there is evidence of good leaf growth I believe in providing the plant with a good thick mulch. This will retain the moisture in the soil in those areas where we have long, dry, hot summers and serve as protection for plants in areas with cold, frosty and even snow covered ground in winter. Mulching has the added advantage of giving good weed control and ease of weeding where control is not perfect. It can also ensure the addition of nutriment to the soil and does provide a most attractive surrounding for the plant.

In my experience a mixture of well rotted duck manure and shavings provides an excellent mulch and this is what we use at Rainbow Ridge with very desirable results. I was first led to this form of mulching by Margaret Lee of Arcadia who grows some of the finest iris and daylilies seen in this state using only this medium for fertilising and mulching. Excellent results can be obtained with other forms of farmyard or stable manure, composted vegetable matter, straw, grass or garden clippings, or purchased mulches and weed inhibitors such as tan bark or spent mushroom compost. Fortunately daylilies are not 'finicky' plants which require precision of pH, so the one important issue for best results is to provide *a* mulch.

While mulching and fertilising are important factors in the after care of any plant, the one single most important factor is water control. Water carries the nutriments in the soil to the roots for absorption and transports the food materials within the plants.

Daylilies are very drought resistant and can survive without heavy watering but for best results they need to be well watered in the spring when the scapes and buds are being formed and particularly in the summer months when in flower. Like most plants they benefit more from a heavy watering 2-3 times per week rather than a quick splash with the hose each day. Watering should be a function of the heat and dryness and the plants should not be over watered to the extent of leaving the ground boggy or leaching nutriment from the soil.

It is best also to avoid overhead watering during the day as the flowers are likely to spot or mark. Early morning or evening watering is by far the most effective and desirable.

Fertilising

Because of their general ease of culture daylilies are often neglected in the fertilising care given in a garden. It is essential to realise that optimum results can only be obtained in optimum conditions and a balanced diet is required for good growth and flowering. Haphazard fertilising is probably better than none at all but care must be taken to avoid an excess of nitrogen. This can result in an abundance of lush foliage and a corresponding decrease in the quantity and quality of flowers. Too much nitrogen often leads to long leggy spikes with small flowers.

Phosphorus is essential to plants coming into flower, particularly if seeds are going to be set. Adequate supplies of phosphorus will help to provide good quality flowers and the best and cheapest source is superphosphate.

Potash is essential for plants to make up a strong, efficient root system and produce good plant increase. Both potassium chloride and potassium sulphate are suitable fertilisers for daylilies.

A satisfactory mulch serves a number of desirable purposes. Straw will reduce weeding and conserve moisture. Compost will perform the above duties and provide some nutriment, but there is a need for more. Animal manures are very useful and if mixed with compost and shavings produce an excellent mulch. The use of a handful of 8-9 month slow release fertiliser at planting time and the addition of a commercial fertiliser in the 5:10:5 ratio in early spring is adequate to give daylilies a good start. Mulching in the summer helps to produce better plants and better autumn bloom. A supplementary late summer dose with a handful of 5:10:5 fertiliser is sufficient for superb all season performance.

It should be realised that each garden is different in its soil composition and requirements and consequently gardeners should develop their own practices and once on to a good system keep with it. Common good sense tells us however that daylily plants will be well served by a feeding straight after initial summer bloom. This will be particularly beneficial to autumn rebloomers as they go through their brief rest period.

Large established clumps should be more heavily fertilised and it is not advisable to fertilise newly planted daylilies until they are established (unless it is with a slow release type fertiliser already mentioned).

Weed control is usually not difficult with established clumps of daylilies as the foliage is dense and close to the ground. Good mulching will further reduce the weed problem and if weeds are kept in check with hand weeding early success in keeping plants clean usually follows. We have experimented with chemical control of summer weeds by using Trifluran compounds such as Treflan with good success. There do not seem to be any problems regarding growth or flowering of the plants but the experiments were not scientifically controlled and while these weed inhibitors are excellent for summer and winter grasses they do not prevent the germination of all weeds.

Good cultivation would require a weekly clean up of the dead or dying outer leaves which can become unsightly, but this is not an essential chore. Many daylily growers get away with a one or two times a year clean up. Of course the dormant cultivars do most of the clean up work for you by dying down in the late autumn and winter and the spent foliage need only then be collected for the compost heap.

Grooming of scapes by removing any dead flowers that have not been pollinated is a desirable, if not essential, chore. Most daylilies are self grooming after 2-3 days, but yesterday's flowers can be unsightly and are best removed if one has the time. This keeps the scape clean and radiant. Pollinated flowers must be left until the seed capsule is clearly visible.

2. PESTS AND DISEASES

Pests

A few years ago I have no doubt that, if asked about pests and diseases that affect daylilies, I would have stated that they are virtually pest and disease free. I don't know whether age has brought greater knowledge, awareness and wisdom or whether the bugs and wogs are catching up with us, but I would now say that daylilies *do* have problems with pests and diseases. Let me hasten to add that they are still an easy-care lazy gardener's plant and relatively pest and disease free. There is no plant that I know that gives as much reward for as little effort. Inevitably if there are insect pests in the garden daylilies will, at least, be partially affected.

Aphids can be a problem, particularly in spring or autumn when the weather is cooler. They feed on the tips of the foliage and often on the young buds, causing foliage to arch over, be malformed and unattractive and leaving buds malformed and even discoloured. There is no doubt that they transmit diseases and are responsible for virus infection. It was not until recent years that I saw a daylily infected by virus but now know that this can happen although the occurrence is rare.

Aphids can be controlled in a variety of ways but I believe that prevention is better than cure. They can be hosed off, washed down with soapy water or sprayed with insecticides. Malathion is a relatively safe contact spray which will kill aphids, but that is the limit of its usage. Metasystox is a far more effective spray as it is systemic, i.e. gets into the system of the plant and has a residual effect of about three weeks. It is, however, a far more dangerous spray to use and has the further disadvantage of a foul and lasting odour. Excellent results have been obtained with Foliomat which is also systemic, has the added advantage of despatching red spider and has no noticeable odour.

Spider Mites can absolutely ravage daylily plants without the gardener having any idea of their presence. These minute insects are not readily observed by the naked eye but they infect lower leaves, eating the chlorophyll and leaving a trail of devastation as they work up the plant. Leaves are left debilitated and unsightly as they brown off and die and plants will not increase or grow well. Red spider, as the most common of these mites is known, is particularly active and increases rapidly in hot dry weather. Growers of daylilies should be warned that Kelthane, though recommended as a standard insecticide for spider mites, can be dangerous to daylily plants and I have heard of growers finding the cure far worse than the complaint when Kelthane is used but I have never used it myself.

Plictran is a safer and more effective controller of red spider and if sprayed regularly on plants will give good control.

The really tough ones will often survive and build up an immunity to sprays so alternate spraying with Foliomat, already mentioned for aphids, is recommended. The unfortunate thing is that once you start spraying and mites build up resistance you have to keep upping the strength of your spray. The ultimate weapon against red spider is Temik (an aldicarb compound) which is highly poisonous if swallowed, inhaled or absorbed through the skin. I would recommend its use only as a last resort but testify to its effectiveness.

If you can resist the temptation to spray, the most natural control of all would be to introduce predatory mites into your garden. These mites feed on the red spider and keep the population down but do not attack the daylilies at all. I know of one New South Wales gardener who uses them very effectively in her extensive daylily plantings and she grows her plants to a very high standard of perfection.

Thrips can also be a problem in late spring or early summer and again in hot dry weather. They do not attack the foliage but can damage the newly opening buds. These insects crawl into the bud and damage the flower leaving white scars on the open blooms which become decidedly unattractive. Control is very difficult and maintaining a good watering programme is my best suggestion. Once thrip is around, the cure is often worse than the complaint as the insecticides used will often only magnify the damage done by the insects. It would seem that Foliomat gives good control of thrip as well as aphids and red spider without any undesirable effects. At the moment it is the best pesticide available for all around protection of daylilies but only time will tell if it will continue to be effective against the insect hordes.

Slugs and snails love to live in the moist protective foliage of daylilies and they really feast on the new soft foliage in the centre of the plant if they are allowed to thrive. They are at their worst in early spring when the plants are making their initial growth. Pelleted or powdered baits such as Baysol or Defender are effective in their control but must be replenished at regular intervals. Care must be taken with household pets and with the application of the powder or pellets to ensure that the snails and slugs actually get to it. Our best results have been obtained with Mesurol which is a more potent form of Baysol, comes as a powder and is mixed up into a spray. By spraying onto the foliage you ensure the Mesurol runs down into the centre of the plant and gives a very effective protection. Of course you have to respray after rain or watering but there is the added advantage of safety for pets. Mesurol and Foliomat are both marketed by Bayer, are compatible for use together, and I would suggest that used together they would just about guarantee pest control.

Nematodes are tiny worms that live in the soil and can on rare occasions be a problem. They attack the roots of many plants but have not been a noticeable problem with daylilies. A 'one off' spraying of the soil with Nemacur will give effective control of nematodes.

There can be passing problems with other biting, sucking or chewing insects but, in general, most leave daylilies alone.

Diseases

Leaf Spot (or **Leaf Streak**) is a fungal disease which shows up as brown markings on the outer leaves. It is unsightly rather than dangerous, is not seen often and is easily controlled by preventative spraying with any mancozeb product such as Dithane.

Soft Rot can occur in wet humid conditions if plants are in poorly drained soil. It is a problem in northern areas where you have the combination of heat and rain, although good positioning of plants reduces it to a very minor problem even under unfavourable climatic conditions. The best treatment is to dig and remove any infected parts and allow the plant to dry out before replanting. A precautionary spray or soaking in an antibiotic such as aureomycin or streptomycin can be helpful.

However, basically, under normal conditions daylilies are disease free.

3. PROPAGATION

Division

The main method of propagation of daylilies is by division. A clump is dug or cut and a plant from the parent is taken and replanted. These divisions will remain true to the original cultivar and this is how daylilies are distributed through nurseries. These divisions can be taken at any time of the year.

Proliferation

Many daylilies will produce small plants from the axils of the scapes. These small plants are called proliferations and if removed and planted will grow true to the parent plant. To produce plants from proliferations cut the scape about 2 cm below the base of the proliferation and establish its roots either by planting directly in the ground or in a mixture of sand and garden soil up to the base of the foliage. Roots are formed very quickly and proliferations will often bloom the following season.

Proliferations seem to occur more readily on diploid cultivars although I have seen them on tetraploids.

Seed

Daylilies can be propagated from seed harvested from deliberately set cross pollinated pods or from bee pods — those set naturally. New cultivars are developed this way and plants raised from seed will not be true to the parent plant although many 'look alikes' will be obtained. Raising daylilies from seed will be discussed more fully in the chapter on hybridising.

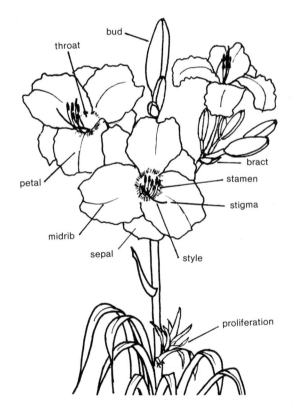

Floral anatomy and parts of a daylily bloom stalk

18

4. LANDSCAPING

When considering landscaping the over-all plan or design is the single most important consideration. It has often concerned me that we have been unable to put into effect landscape ideas that would have so much appeal and it is only in recent times that I have thought that it would be possible to run a commercial business and have a nicely landscaped garden as well. So part of the next 'five year plan' at Rainbow Ridge is to landscape with iris and daylilies while still attempting to keep the commercial side of the property going.

Whatever the plants to be used, the design comes first and the planting is there to accentuate and bring the design to life. As such, the plants, in this case the daylilies, to be used should be fitted into the overall design whether they are to be the dominant plants in the landscape design or just used as focal points. Of course a garden plan could involve the use of daylilies and no other plants. It could be a collector's garden all set out in alphabetical order or according to colour, either blending or contrasting.

A massed effect can be obtained by planting quite a few daylilies in one section of the garden and here careful thought must be given to the type of growth, the vigour and the bloom period before a final selection, which is often mistakenly made on colour alone, is made.

Most gardeners would not wish to landscape with hemerocallis alone and would be looking to grow their daylilies as companion plants with other favourites or have other plants to act as companions for their favourite daylilies.

Landscaping with Daylilies

In the introduction I have outlined many of the popular plants that can be grown in conjunction with daylilies and the possibilities for use with these and other plants are as varied as the imagination of the landscaper. In this chapter I would like to outline just a few ideas on how these wonderful plants could be used and a few of the colour combinations of my own favourite cultivars that come to mind.

The successful use of roses and hemerocallis can create a stunning garden picture. Imagine a beautiful white background of a wall or trellis covered with the climbing rose 'Shot Silk', underplanted with the lovely floribunda rose 'Elizabeth of Glamis' and then further underplanted with the delightful pale cream diploid daylily 'So Lovely' or the soft ruffled pink tetraploid daylily 'Ballet'. Of course the combinations are endless and there are so many other daylilies that could be used. The beautiful ruffled melon apricot tetraploid 'Alison' would be a worthy substitute for the above.

I could imagine nothing nicer than a short walkway set out pergola style and covered

Landscaping with daylilies

with the remontant single red climbing rose 'Altissimo' and underplanted with the tall bright red tetraploid hemerocallis 'Apple Tart'. What a combination! Suitable substitutes would be the dark red diploid 'Fannie Stadler', the bright red diploid 'Passion' or the sensational new reds 'Scarlock', 'Christmas Day' and 'James Marsh'.

'Pink Parfait' has always been a favourite rose of mine with its healthy clean foliage, multitude of flowers and quick repetition of bloom. I could imagine a bed of 'Pink Parfait' roses edged with the magnificent pink tetraploid daylily 'Round Table' or the even softer pink coloured near white tetraploid 'Pearl Island' or the bright ruffled pink beauty 'Dancing Shiva'.

Another top rose for flower production quantity and quality is 'Red Gold' a rich golden yellow heavily edged red. Reds and yellows abound in daylilies and a bed of 'Red Gold' could be edged in the rich gold of 'By Myself', a superb daylily, the reds already mentioned for use with 'Altissimo', or a red and yellow daylily such as 'Spanish Brocade'. In the yellow daylilies the evergreens 'Chrome Lemon' or 'California Butterfly' could be used, or some of the excellent dormants like 'Creepy Crawler', 'Dorethe Louise', 'Double Jackpot', 'Gleeman Song', 'Golden Milestone', 'Golden Prize', 'Golden Surrey' or 'Mary Todd'. Colour combination for rose beds and daylilies combined are endless and the only restriction is your imagination.

Pathways and driveways are excellent sites for hemerocallis. I can remember the delight of a colleague when he was given 50 plants of the tall red copper and gold evergreen tetraploid 'Chanticleer' to use along a difficult stretch of driveway. The edging was right, the height was right, the colour attractive and on view for many months in the year and, of course, the growth on a cultivar like 'Chanticleer' is superb.

A stunning edging to a driveway could be obtained by planting the magnificent evergreen 'Chinese Autumn' which grows to about 80 cm (2½ feet) and is a consistent rebloomer. The heavily pleated and ruffled flowers are a pastel yet brilliant blend of coral orange and apricot and they absolutely glow. Because the plant habit is so tidy this is an excellent bordering daylily. Equally superb for edging is the dormant cultivar 'Flames of Fortune', another prolific bloomer, similar in height to 'Chinese Autumn' and carrying flowers of irridescent ivory cream to melon with a pink throat. No matter what your choice, daylilies are great edgers and many would favour having clumps of quite a few different cultivars to edge their paths. Daylilies for edging plants could be used alone or in conjunction with other perennials or annuals. They could be used as a solid border or in spot plantings to highlight a path.

Daylilies are excellent soil retainers and they can be used very effectively to bind the soil and prevent erosion. As such, they are excellent plants for use on difficult slopes where they will maintain the soil and present an opportunity for effective underplanting. Again they are superb along the edges of lakes or ponds where they can be used as a dominant planting or to give accent in spot plantings.

As a perennial to be used for effect near a pool the daylily can be matched only by the iris and why not be brave and use both. A lovely effect can be achieved by the planting of one single clump of a daylily cultivar positioned so that the flowers are reflected in the pool. Which hemerocallis do you use — the choice is up to you. For the author the choice would be painful. It more or less poses the question of what is your favourite daylily and for me this varies from day to day and usually ends up with the one that is out and looking best at the time.

Daylilies are excellent in massed bedding around a single focus such as a large tree or sundial or some other garden feature such as a statue or gazebo. Whether you plant in a circle, rectangle or square, or irregularly is a matter of personal choice, just as it is personal choice whether you plant one or several different cultivars. Again care must be taken with regard to growth, height of scape, flowering time and colour patterns if a pleasing overall effect is to be obtained.

The Cottage Garden

As a so called old fashioned plant hemerocallis have their place in the cottage garden, which was one of the first types of garden developed in Australia and very much in the English tradition. Just as the daylily is enjoying a return to favour, so is the cottage garden going through a period of great popularity. In a cottage garden spectacular eye catching impact is sacrificed for the delicate, even fragile, beauty of old fashioned plants.

A cottage garden is an easy care garden, informal by nature and showing colour throughout the year. It features a minimum of shrubs and a maximum of perennials, annuals and ground covers, accentuated by plantings of bulbs and herbs.

The climatic conditions will determine the most suitable plants for a cottage garden and it is not the intention of the author to go into any plant selection detail. Among many books that go into such matters in depth I can recommend Trevor Nottle's *Growing Perennials*, a companion volume in the same series as this text.

Daylilies as Pot Plants

Daylilies are very suitable plants for pot culture and plants grown in containers can be used very effectively on account of the length

Landscaping with daylilies

Daylilies in pots

and continuity of bloom and the fact that the container may be moved into a variety of suitable positions during the growing season.

As the typical daylily plant makes a thick mat of roots quite quickly they are best planted in large containers or tubs. It is my experience that single plants or double divisions in 20 cm (8") pots will grow nicely and flower well in their first year. Even the weaker growers are pot bound after one season and although bloom is good in the second season they would then have to be potted on. We have used 20 cm (8") pots as a basis for nursery sales and although I know of people using smaller containers the plants that are put into them are invariably very small. I would suggest that the home gardener should be looking at a minimum of a 30 cm (12") tub for effective and continuous container cultivation.

Containers used should be deep to allow an adequate root run, should be well drained by using a suitable material such as old broken terracotta pots as a basis and should be filled to within 2-3 cm of the top with a well composted soil mix low in nitrogen. Slight acidity is preferred, so a 1:1:1 mix of good garden soil, peat moss and well rotted manure would give an excellent medium. Ensure that adequate room is left at the top of the pot to facilitate watering and the application of a suitable mulch.

Plants suitable for use in containers would vary according to taste but I would favour the low growing cultivars and would not consider using the very tall cultivars.

Low Growing Cultivars

'**Ann Blocher**' This orchid to lilac pink with a mauve influence gradually lightens during the day to a creamy white with a rose to mauve edge in the afternoon. The medium sizes flowers are perfectly formed and heavily ruffled and in proportion to the 50 cm (20") scapes. This daylily flowers early and then reblooms, is semi-evergreen in most climates and is a favourite of the author. It is a very recent import from the U.S.A. and is still quite expensive but well worth the initial outlay. (Plate 20)

'**Archangel**' is a beautiful light orange melon toned daylily of exquisite form and ruffle. It is a dormant cultivar which flowers mid season and produces its beautiful blooms on 55 cm (22") scapes.

'**Blessed Trinity**' is a superb container plant. The near white flowers show a little cream and a green throat. They are well formed, medium sized, nicely ruffled and come in profusion on low 50 cm (20") scapes. The plants are semi-evergreen but would be evergreen in tropical climates and they flower early and then repeat. This is a joy to grow. (Plate 49)

'**Butter Gold**' is a superb daylily. This one was bred in Australia by Barry Blyth and the name describes the colour. The blooms are heavily substanced, diamond dusted and ruffled. They are held on 60 cm (24") scapes and flower early and continuously throughout the season. 'Butter Gold' is a dormant tetraploid.

'**Call to Remembrance**' is another near white and really gives a white effect in the garden. The creamy flowers have a green throat and are held on very low 40 cm (16") scapes. The flowers are 12.5 cm (5") in diameter, well formed and ruffled. This daylily is an early bloomer and semi-evergreen in most climates. (Plate 76)

'**Chicago Weathermaster**' has for a long while been our favourite purple. The large ruffled flowers are a smooth medium purple with a green throat. They come early in the season on low 50 cm (20") scapes. This daylily is a dormant tetraploid.

'**Dancing Shiva**' is another great low growing cultivar. The scapes are 55 cm (22") high and the plant is a semi-evergreen tetraploid which flowers early with some rebloom. The flowers are spectacular. A soft blue pink in colour, they are perfectly rounded, circular with wide overlapping petals all ruffled and crimped at the edges. (Plate 24)

'**Etched in Gold**' is a beautiful pastel primrose yellow and pink blend with a frilly gold edge. This dormant tetraploid is a good grower and prolific bloomer. The scapes reach 50 cm (20") in height. (Plate 54)

'**Full Welcome**' is a real favourite. The low 50 cm (20") scapes carry large 19 cm (7½") flowers in a clear light, bright yellow. Flowers are ruffled and beautifully formed. 'Full Welcome' is a dormant tetraploid.

'**Hope Diamond**' is a beautiful cream ruffled daylily about 10 cm (4") in diameter on very low 35 cm (14") scapes. It flowers early and reblooms on a dormant plant.

'**La Charmante**' is an excellent daylily. The large broad petalled and wide flowers are rose pink with a large creamy yellow circular throat which looks spectacular. The low growing scapes are 60 cm (24") and the plant is an evergreen tetraploid.

'**La Peche**' is another excellent daylily in apricot, peach tones. The flowers are all ruffled, frilly and laced and the plant is a low growing 60 cm (24") tetraploid which is evergreen. (Plate 79)

'**Scottish Belle**' is one of the best pinks. It is a low growing 50 cm (20") plant, dormant and tetraploid. The beautifully ruffled and well formed flowers are a rose pink blend.

'**Short Stuff**' is an everpopular daylily as the scapes are a mass of bloom. It is a superb pot plant and a landscaper's dream. This is a very short growing daylily reaching only 40 cm (16") in height. The plants are evergreen and it is tetraploid. The large, wide, ruffled flowers are dawn pink with rose pink halo and chartreuse throat.

'**Summer Wine**' is a spectacular 15 cm (6") flower on a low 60 cm (24") scape. The dormant plants carry masses of heavily ruffled, crimped and overlapping petals in an unique colour of clear grape violet with a greenish yellow heart. This is a very good daylily for container or garden. (Plate 98)

All of the above are excellent landscape or specimen daylilies as well as being suitable for container culture.

If a taller plant is desired there is no reason for not using it and every reason for using it if it suits the position and the gardener's wishes.

5. CLASSIFICATION

Foliage habit

As already mentioned daylilies can be classified according to foliage habit. Some are evergreen; they retain their foliage throughout the year and are most suited to northern climates.

Others are dormant; they lose their foliage completely in the colder months only to send up new foliage in spring. These are best grown in the southern states of Australia and the south island of New Zealand. Finally there are those that are classified as semi-evergreen (which could just as well be called semi-dormant); their foliage dies back part way and, after a resting period in the colder months, grows again in spring.

It is difficult to give a ruling on which daylilies suit which climate other than the generalisation above, but potential growers should realise that there are many exceptions to the rule and mostly on the positive side; that is, virtually all evergreens are excellent in tropical climates but many dormants grow well also, and virtually all dormants are excellent in colder climates but many of the evergreens grow equally well. Do not be put off by the foliage habit if you fancy a particular daylily but talk about it to your specialist nurseryman or other growers in your area or be brave, take the initiative and try it yourself. Remember that most reputable nurserymen who deal in daylilies (as in iris) will give you a guarantee with your plant.

Daylilies will acclimatise to conditions with which they are unfamiliar or which are basically unsuitable for them and often they acclimatise very quickly. Never judge a daylily on its first year performance. They usually take a year to settle in and even though some will give a good performance in their first year they are always better in their second year.

Tetraploids

Our next means of classification is whether a daylily is diploid or tetraploid and unless you are interested in hybridising, for which this is essential knowledge, I would not allow this to be a major concern. I have, at times, separated the diploids and tetraploids in the garden but now doubt the wisdom of this. Indeed, unless told, most growers, even specialists, would not be able to tell the difference between the two types.

A diploid contains the basic number of chromosomes for the species in each cell. The hemerocallis species has 22 chromosomes. By the use of a chemical substance, colchicine, the number of chromosomes has been doubled to 44. It is these chromosomes, minute particles in the nucleus of the cell, which determine the characteristics of a plant. When two plants are hybridised the seed produced will contain chromosomes from both parents and it is this genetic combination which determines the characteristics of the new plant developed from the seed. The chances of daylilies coming 'true' to either of their parents are very small and the higher the chromosome number the greater will be the diversity. In the late 1930s the chemical colchicine was found to be able to double the chromosome number and it was used to induce 44 chromosome, better known as tetraploid, daylilies. This was a whole new race with many advantages over the diploids apart from the obvious greater diversity in inherited properties for the hybridisers to work on.

Tetraploid daylilies are larger stronger plants with better substanced foliage and increased vigour in leaf and stem. The scapes produced are stronger and the flowers are larger, more intense in colour and very much improved in substance. Top quality tetraploid daylilies are outstanding achievements of hybridisation and it is in this 'new race' that the future of the daylily lies.

However, let it be clearly understood that, at this stage, the hybridising of diploid daylilies has reached such a high standard that the better diploids more than compare with the average tetraploids and it is only the best of the tetraploids which are clearly on a different plane. These new hybrids are coming mainly from the United States of America and are very expensive plants, costing up to US$200 per plant on introduction. At current rates of exchange this places them at over A$300 to import and up to near NZ$400, so they are beyond the budget of the average gardener. Fortunately Australian nurserymen are prepared to pay these huge prices to get top quality plants into the country and offer them to customers at a fraction of these prices and, even more important, use this stock to develop a local breeding campaign. This is having the desired effect as many outstanding cultivars are being developed here.

Height

The one further point of plant classification is the height of the flowering scape. The scapes are simply categorised as low, medium or tall. Low indicates up to 60 cm (24"), medium 60 cm — 90 cm (24" — 36") and tall over 90 cm (36"). Scapes under 30 cm (12") are often called 'dwarf' and this can be misleading as dwarf applies only to height of scape and the flowers may be quite large. Growing heights given in this book are generally as registered by the hybridiser unless there are striking anomalies when the plant is grown in our climate. They can only be a guide because height of scape will vary from one location to another, from one season to another and even according to position in the garden.

A good example of this is the very popular red 'Apple Tart'. This daylily is registered at 70 cm (28") in the U.S.A., usually grows taller here, but in 1986 a magnificent clump at Rainbow Ridge carried in excess of 60 scapes all over 120 cm (48") high. The few tallest scapes were 150 cm (60") high, more than twice the registered height, yet I would recommend 'Apple Tart' as a medium grower for height of scape.

The Flower

In evaluating the daylily flower there are four major criteria (1) the size (2) the form (3) the pattern and (4) the colour. There are also other aspects of the daylily flower worth noting; these include blooming habit, blooming time in the season and such characteristics as substance, texture, and veining.

Size
There are three categories for size in daylilies

(1) miniature, where the flowers are less than 7.5 cm (3") in diameter; (2) small flowered, where the flowers are between 7.5 cm (3") and 11 cm (4½") in diameter; and (3) large flowered, where the flowers are more than 11 cm (4½") in diameter. Some of the large flowered cultivars have blooms in excess of 20 cm (8") and I have seen blooms measuring 25 cm (10") in diameter. It is normal, although not essential, to have flower size in proportion to the height of the scape. I would find miniature flowers on towering scapes somewhat difficult to appreciate, but do find large flowers on low scapes quite attractive as long as the flowers are held above the foliage.

Form

The daylily flower may be single, double or semi double. The typical flower consists of six parts; the three larger parts set to the front of the flower are called petals, while the other three parts, usually smaller, are called sepals. Most daylily blooms have three petals and three sepals and are called single. Sometimes the blooms have a few extra petaloids and these blooms are called semi-double. Flowers with more than six segments are called double. The double daylilies themselves take different forms with the extra segments appearing as a tuft of petals in the middle of the flower or as an extra layer or layers of petals. The extent to which 'double' daylilies are, in fact, double will be seen to vary and there are often anomalies in garden performance as well. Some doubles are always double; others are often single for the first season then fully and continuously double once established; while others again are single early in the season and double on repeat bloom.

Having dispensed with doubles let us now look at the various different forms of the single bloom.

Circular

Circular or **rounded** form is very desirable and pleasing. The flowers have a circular outline, usually with overlapping segments to give a full effect. The segments are short and wide.

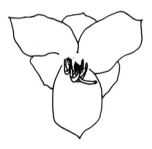

Triangular

Triangular form exists when the segments form the basic outline of two overlapping triangles with vertices pointing in opposite directions. The sepals usually recurve.

Double

Star

Recurved

Star shaped form exists when the segments tend to be long and pointed with a considerable space in between them, giving the effect of a six pointed star.

Spider

Spider form exists when the length of the segments is five times (or more) the width. A true 'spider' should conform to these standards, but there are many 'spider form' daylilies on the market which are neither one thing nor the other. Spiders, like doubles, can be considered another class of daylily altogether and they have their admirers.

All of the above are easily discernible as you look into the flower but there are certain characteristics observed by looking at the flower from the side.

Flowers are said to be **flaring** when the segments arch out from the throat as if stretched.

Flowers are said to be **flat** when nearly all of the segments sit roughly in the same plane except, of course, for the throat of the flower.

Recurved flowers will basically flare only to have the outer part of the segments roll back beneath the inner parts giving a tucked in effect.

Trumpet form is when the segments continue to rise from the throat in an upward line to the point. The parts tend to form the rim of a cup at the outer extremities.

Pinched

A pinched flower is where the petal is in two planes and looks as though someone has held the flower between two fingers.

Ruffled

A ruffled flower has a rippled edge to its petals.

28

The length and width of the daylily flower parts vary, to give the shapes described above, from the extremely narrow, open flowered spiders to those which are extremely wide petalled. The sepals are invariably more narrow than the petals and at times we have the pin wheel effect of petals which twist and curl. To all these qualities we can add the distinction of plain (tailored) floral parts or ruffled floral parts. These parts can be fluted or have crimped edges. Even the extent of this ruffling, fluting and crimping can vary and some cultivars such as the beautiful 'Chicago Knobby' carry extra adornments in the form of slightly raised knobs the size of the head of a pin. There is endless variation to the flower form and each cultivar has its own distinctive appearance.

Another amazing habit of daylilies is the way the form varies throughout the day as well as from day to day. Perhaps the best example of this is the spectacular 'Ida Wimberly Munson' which opens very much in a cup shaped, trumpet form and gradually flattens out during the day, whereupon the sepals tend to slightly recurve while the petals take on a triangular shape. This daylily flower goes through quite a variety of shapes in its brief existence and it is beautiful at all stages.

Pattern

As well as characteristic forms daylilies have characteristic patterns of application of colour. There are six recognised different colour patterns, but there are subdivisions within these divisions and combinations which make it difficult to categorise the colour patterns. Further and continuous development will, no doubt, further widen this means of classification.

The six basic patterns are (1) self (2) blend (3) polychrome (4) bitone (5) bicolour (6) eye-zone.

A self flower is one in which all the floral parts are of the same single colour.

A blended flower is one in which all the floral parts are of two basic colours or shades of colour.

A polychrome flower is one in which all the floral parts are a mixture of three or more colours or shades of colour.

A bitone flower has sepals of one colour and petals a different shade of the same colour. If the sepals are lighter than the petals it is called a bitone; if the sepals are darker than the petals it is called a reverse bitone.

A bicolour flower has sepals of one colour and petals a different colour. If the sepals are lighter than the petals it is called a bicolour, if the sepals are darker than the petals a reverse bicolour.

An eye zone is a pattern in addition to all the above patterns and all the above may or may not have an eye zone, which is a solid 'ring' of colour at the junction of the floral segments and the throat. In itself the eye zone can take a variety of forms. The term **eye zone** is used if this ring of colour is on both sepals and petals. If it is only on the petals it is called a **band.** If it is only slight or barely visible it is called a **halo.** If it is very wide and stretches out over most of the floral parts it is called a **watermark.** The terms eye zone, band, halo and watermark are all indicative of a ring of colour on the floral parts, but each is indicative of a different type of application of this ring.

As well as the six basic colour patterns and variations on the ring effect there are numerous other applications of colour. These take the form of edging, midrib colour, tipping and dusting.

Some daylilies have the segments edged in a colour or shade different to that of the basic parts. This **edging** varies from the thinnest of wire lines to the clearest, defined lines of up to 1 cm in width. Colour combinations vary greatly as does the intensity of the colour of this edging.

Some daylilies develop a line of colour down the length of the segments. This is called a **midrib** and in some cultivars this midrib is raised above the surface of the rest of the segments. Midrib colours vary, often blending with the main colour and sometimes contrasting vividly.

Some daylilies have the ends or tips of the segments a different colour to the main part of the segments. This **tipping** can occur on the petals only or on both sepals and petals.

Another common adornment to daylily flowers is the **dusting** effect where the whole surface of the floral parts is minutely dotted with colour flashes. This dusting takes the form of 'gold dusting', where the flowers reflect the light and give a gold sparkle, or 'diamond dusting' where the effect is similar but in tones of silver. Either way this is a spectacular addition of colour and most daylilies showing this effect are highly prized.

Colour

The colour range of the daylily flower has been extended to cover all basic colours with the exception of blue and pure white. From the original species in shades of yellow and orange there is now a full range of yellow colours from the palest lemon (near white) to the richest gold, and a full range in orange tones with brown, melon, apricot and tangerine. Reds of all shades are available, through orange red, brick red, scarlet, pillar box red, maroon and burgundy to those near black from the red side. Again in pink there is a full range of colours from the palest pink (near white) through to rich rose pink, and in purple from lilac, lavender, mauve and violet through to rich royal purples, plum coloured and black grape from the purple side. The search for blue continues with only minor advances being made but the goal of a clear white is very close to being reached.

Added to the colour of the floral parts in all the patterns already discussed, daylilies often have a different coloured throat and sometimes right in the centre of the flower, called the heart, another colour again. The throat and heart colours may contrast or blend with the principal colour and may be minute or extend visibly onto the floral parts. It is only when petal colour, throat and heart are all identical that we have a complete self and this occurs only in the yellow shades with very few exceptions.

A further colour variation can occur in the stamens — the six male parts — which are usually yellow but can vary in colour to be red, black, pink or shades of mauve.

6. PURCHASING PLANTS

Daylilies grow so well universally that prospective buyers need only consider what type of daylily to purchase if they live in climatic extremes. Gardeners in hot tropical climates would be well advised to consider only evergreen cultivars initially, while those who live in cold climates would be best served by dormant cultivars.

Intending buyers will often be able to obtain unnamed or very old cultivars from non-specialist nurseries at bargain prices and this may be very satisfactory for someone who wishes to just fill a spot in the garden. Price should be a guide to quality and new release daylilies are an expensive proposition. First release cultivars in the United States vary in price from about US$40 (A$60, NZ$80) upward to US$200 (A$300, NZ$400) with an averge price around the US$75 (A$110, NZ$150) mark. These are not cheap plants and importing nurseries pay for certification, packing, freight and quarantine fees. Fortunately daylilies are relatively disease free and very tough, so losses are not usually experienced. Most grow quickly so they are often able to be released within two years of importing, but even then prices must of necessity be high and new releases in Australia are often in the $25 to $50 bracket. Price is then determined by supply and demand and many top quality daylilies can be purchased from specialist nurseries at prices in the $6 to $10 bracket. I would always recommend dealing with a specialist nurseryman as he can provide a service unavailable elsewhere and any extra cost, if indeed there is any, is money well spent.

Plants should not conform to any predetermined size as they make up very quickly and most nurserymen will supply a double division to ensure satisfaction if stock allows. The supply of new cultivars is often very limited, so smaller plants and single divisions are often all that is supplied of new releases.

Try to get to see flowers in bloom at specialist nurseries or in the gardens of friends who live in your area and, failing this, rely on the advice of your specialist nurseryman. New cultivars are being bred in Australia and released at moderate prices. Many of these are equal to and superior to the latest overseas cultivars. In presenting a list of recommended cultivars I have tried to nominate those tried and tested quality daylilies which will always be worth a place in the garden. I have not included very old cultivars or those not readily available; I have included quite a few very recent or new cultivars which have outstanding characteristics, although I recognise that these may be outside the price range of many prospective daylily growers. In general, the recommended cultivars will be available from one or more of the specialist nurserymen listed on page 55. If you order through the mail your plants may arrive looking dry. They should be soaked overnight (8-10 hours) in water or a weak solution of liquid fertiliser such as Aquasol.

Recommended Cultivars

In this section the following abbreviations are used:
Ev. — Evergreen, E. — Early,
Min. — Miniature, S.Ev. — Semi-evergreen,
M. — Midseason, Tet. — Tetraploid,
Dor. — Dormant, L. — Late, Dip. — Diploid,
Re. — Rebloom.

Sizes are given in inches as daylilies are still registered this way. The first size is the height of the scape, the second the diameter of the flower. All flowers not named as tetraploid can be assumed to be diploid.

'Absalon' Ev. 28" Tet. Ruffled creamy yellow with a pink flush. Strong and prolific.

'Aisha' Ev. 24" M. Re. Tet. Large pastel peach of superb form, texture and stems. Great rebloom for us. A super daylily.

'Alison' Dor. 28" M. Tet. Large 6" flowers are ruffled peach pink on excellent scapes. (Plate 13)

'Amber Lamp' Ev. E. M. 26" Dip. Pastel amber, reblooms.

'Ann Blocher' S.Ev. 20" E. M. Dip. Re. Words can't describe this beauty — rosy violet with white hints giving the best blue violet effect so far. (Plate 20)

'Apple Tart' Ev. 28" Re. Tet. Super ruffled mid to dark red with a green throat. Quick increase. Top daylily. (Plate 77)

'Archangel' Dor. 22" M. L. Dip. Lovely light orange melon with a raised midrib and yellow heart. Blooms open wide.

'Astarte' Ev. 26" E. M. Re. Tet. Broad ruffled pastel 5" flowers in ivory, cream and pink. Quick to increase. (Plate 39)

'Aviance' Ev. 24" E. M. Tet. Broad ruffled creamy pink. Super quality.

'Aztec Autumn' S.Ev. 30" M. Tet. Blend of orange, coral and peach.

'Ballet' Ev. 30" M. Re. Tet. Broad, ruffled rose pink of good form and growth. (Plate 30)

'Balls of Red' Dor. 30" M. Re. Dip. Double light red which is floriferous and reliable. (Plate 53)

'Bells Appealing' Dor. E. M. 28" Re. Tet. Beautiful mid yellow flowers are large, wide, overlapping and ruffled.

'Bengaleer' Dor. 36" Tet. Very large rich deep yellow flowers reach 7½" in diameter. Excellent growth.

'Binnorie' Dor. 32" Tet. Smooth blended pink, green yellow throat. Large 6" flowers.

'Bishop's Crest' Ev. 36" Tet. E. M. and continuous rebloom. Tall spikes carry broad ruffled silvery mauve flowers with a bold purple eye throughout the season. (Plate 16)

'Blessed Trinity' S.Ev. 20" E. Re. Dip. Very close to the elusive white, greenish throat. A super daylily. (Plate 49)

'Bold Baron' Dor. 27" Tet. Large light purple flowers with a striking broad white stripe down the centre of the petals.

'Bold One' S.Ev. 40" M. Dip. Very large and showy bright gold with a large purple eye and yellow throat. Spectacular.

'Boss' Ev. 28" E. M. Re. Tet. Large melon, lavender midribs, green throat.

'Botticelli' Ev. 32" E. M. Tet. Very large deep pink, gold throat.

'Boundless Love' Ev. 28" M. Pretty pale pink, close to white. Lovely form.

'Bouquet of Ruffles' Ev. 26" M. Re. Tet. My favourite pink! Round ruffled and full clear pink of excellent form and growth. (Plate 99)

'Braided Satin' Dor. 29" M. Tet. Broad rounded soft creamy pink.

'Buddhist Flame' Ev. 28" E. M. Tet. Bright coral orange red with a gold throat. Heavily ruffled flowers.

'Butter Gold' Dor. 24" E. M. Tet. Re. Super butter gold self all diamond dusted and ruffled.

'Butterscotch Ripples' Dor. M. 32" Tet. Creamy yellow with a tan overlay and gold edge. Ruffled flowers.

'By Myself' Dor. 32" M. Re. Tet. Large ruffled gold with broad rounded petals. Blooms continually. (Plate 22)

'California Butterfly' Ev. 36" E. Re. Tet. Very large, showy bright canary yellow self. Well formed ruffled 7" flowers. Excellent.

1. 'James Marsh' (p.51)

2. Daylily planting at Rainbow Ridge

3. 'Naomi Ruth' (miniature) (p.53)

4. 'Child Bride' (p.49)

5. 'Little Green Apples' (small flowered miniature) (p.52)
(*Photo:* Barry Blyth)

6. 'Round Table' (p.53)

7. 'Elizabeth Anne Hudson' (p.50)

8. 'Music of Love' (p.52) bred in Australia by Barry Blyth (*Photo:* Barry Blyth)

9. 'My Ways' (p.52)

10. 'Cinnamon Roll' (p.49)

11. 'Embassy' (p.50)

12. 'Elizabethan Love' (*Photo:* Barry Blyth)

13. 'Alison' (p.32)

14. 'Douglas Dale' (p.50)

15. 'Cindy Marie' (*Photo:* Barry Blyth)

16. 'Bishop's Crest' (p.32)

17. 'Delightful Eyeful' (*Photo:* Barry Blyth)

18. 'Chinese Autumn' (p.49)

19. 'Alma Cangemi' (*Photo:* Barry Blyth)

20. 'Ann Blocher' (pp.23 & 32)

21. 'Angel Tears'

22. 'By Myself' (p.32)

23. 'Lord Camden' (p.52) (*Photo:* Barry Blyth)

24. 'Dancing Shiva' (pp.24 & 50)

25. 'Dancer' (p.50)

26. 'El Tigre' (p.50)

27. 'Cordon Rouge' (p.49)

28. 'Dress Circle' (p.50)

29. 'Chicago Brave' (p.49)

30. 'Ballet' (p.32)

31. 'Doll House' (p.50) (*Photo:* Barry Blyth)

32. 'Olive Bailey Langdon' (p.53)

33. 'Pouter Pigeon'

34. 'Folklorico' (p.50)

35. 'Ming Treasure' (p.52)

36. 'Hope Diamond' (p.51)

37. 'Mary Todd' (p.52)

38. 'Malaysian Spice' (p.52)

39. 'Astarte' (p.32)

40. 'Highland Lass' (p.51)

41. 'Feathered Friend' (p.50)

42. 'Indonesia' (p.51) (*Photo:* Barry Blyth)

43. 'Golden Milestone' (p.51)

44. 'Ida Wimberly Munson' (p.51)

45. 'Topaz Glow' bred in Australia by Margaret Lee

46. 'Grape Velvet' (p.51)

47. 'Heather Green (p.51)

48. 'Commandment' (p.49)

49. 'Blessed Trinity' (pp.23 & 32)

50. 'Mask Ball' (p.52) (*Photo:* Barry Blyth)

51. 'Double Talk' (p.50)

52. 'Double Razzle Dazzle' (*Photo:* Barry Blyth)

53. 'Balls of Red' (p.32)

54. 'Etched in Gold' (pp.24 & 50)

55. 'Dwarf King' (miniature)

56. 'Siloam Fairy Tale' (miniature) (p.54)
(*Photo:* Barry Blyth)

57. 'Green Dragon' (semi-spider) (p.51)

58. 'Red Thrill (spider) (*Photo:* courtesy of Trevor Nottle)

41

59. 'Eternal Blessing' (p.50) (*Photo:* Barry Blyth)

60. 'Sir Oliver' (p.54) (*Photo: Barry Blyth)*

61. 'Seductress' (p.54) (*Photo:* Barry Blyth)

62. 'Real Wind' (p.53)

63. 'Green Glade' (p.51)

64. 'Venetian Magistrate' (p.54) (*Photo:* Barry Blyth)

65. 'Russian Rhapsody' (p.53)

66. 'Pass Me Not' (p.53)

67. 'Royal Blue Blood' (*Photo:* Barry Blyth)

68. 'Searching Love' (*Photo:* Barry Blyth)

69. 'Veiled Magic' (p.54)

70. 'Quinn Buck' (p.53)

71. 'Valedictorian' (p.54)

72. 'My Rosary' (p.52)

73. 'Yasmin' (p.55)

74. Massed daylily display at Tempo Two Nursery
(*Photo:* Barry Blyth)

75. 'Bertie Ferris' (miniature) (*Photo:* Barry Blyth)

76. 'Call to Remembrance' (pp.23 & 49)

77. 'Apple Tart' (p.32)

78. 'Spring Sunrise' (*Photo:* Barry Blyth)

79. 'La Peche' (pp24 & 52)

80. 'Meadow Mystic' (p.52)

81. 'Renaissance Fair' (p.53)

82. 'Paper Lanterns' (*Photo:* Barry Blyth)

83. 'Gallant Eyes' (miniature) (p.50)
(*Photo:* Barry Blyth)

84. 'Chicago Star' (p.49)

85. 'Tovarich' (p.54)

86. 'Simply Pretty' (p.54)

87. 'Astolat'

88. 'Fair Annet'

89. 'Ginger Jar' (p.51)

90. Daylily display at Rainbow Ridge

91. 'Jane Austen' (p.51)

92. 'Regal Tapestry' (p.53) (*Photo:* Barry Blyth)

93. 'Dorethe Louise' (p.50)

94. Daylilies at Rainbow Ridge

95. 'Flames of Fortune' (p.50)

96. 'Scarlock' (p.54)

97. 'Chemistry' (p.49) Bred in Australia
by Barry Blyth (*Photo:* Barry Blyth)

98. 'Summer Wine' (p.24)

99. 'Bouquet of Ruffles' (p.32)

100. 'Higashi' (p.51)

'**Call to Remembrance**' S.Ev. 16" E. M. Dip. Creamy white with a green throat. Low, well branched and ruffled 5" blooms. (Plate 76)

'**Camden Charm**' M. 18" Rounded 3" blooms of pale pink, chartreuse throat. Ruffled.

'**Capella Light**' Ev. 28" E. M. Tet. Re. Creamy opal yellow blooms are large, ruffled and beautifully formed. Top quality.

'**Cenla Crepe Myrtle**' 30" E. M. Dip. Creped and ruffled light pink.

'**Central Park**' Dor. E. M. L. 22" Tet. Large dark ruffled red with crepe velvet texture.

'**Chamonix**' Ev. 30" E. M. Re. Ruffled and overlapping rose pink with excellent branching.

'**Champagne Taffy**' Dor. 20" E. M. Dip. Diamond dusted champagne coloured blooms with wide overlapping petals. Nice.

'**Chandigarh**' S.Ev. 32" M. Tet. Lavender mauve edged ivory lavender. Bright bold blue lavender eye.

'**Chateau Blanc**' Ev. 26" M. L. Re. Tet. Round ruffled and crimped ivory cream with a delicate gold wire edge. Super daylily.

'**Chemistry**' Ev. 30" E. M. Re. Tet. The best daylily bred in Australia to date! A medley of autumn tones, coral, salmon and apricot with a golden apricot throat. Superior growth and prolific bloom with all the top qualities of its great parent 'Chinese Autumn'. (Plate 97)

'**Cherry Lace**' Dor. 36" M. Re. Dip. Heavily ruffled cherry rose with a green throat. Long blooming season.

'**Chicago Blackout**' S.Ev. 30" M. Tet. Black red with a green throat. Heavy bloom.

'**Chicago Brave**' Dor. 28" M. Tet. Heavily ruffled dark red blooms with crimped edge. Super quality. (Plate 29)

'**Chicago Heather**' Dor. 28" E. M. Tet. Re. Large 6" ruffled lavender blooms. Creamy green throat.

'**Chicago Knobby**' S.Ev. 22" E. M. Tet. Purple bitone, heavily ruffled flowers with tiny raised knobs on the petals.

'**Chicago Rosy**' Dor. 25" E. M. Tet. Ruffled dark rosy pink to light rosy red. Large 6½" flowers.

'**Chicago Silky**' Dor. 25" M. Tet. Re. Super ruffled coral pink. Exquisite form.

'**Chicago Silver**' Dor. 30" E. M. Tet. Beautiful large ruffled clear silver purple with all segments edged in white.

'**Chicago Star**' Dor. 24" M. Tet. Star shaped light golden yellow with a green throat. (Plate 84)

'**Chicago Two Bits**' Dor. 26" M. Tet. Clear light purple, creamy green throat. Large ruffled flowers.

'**Chicago Weathermaster**' Dor. 20" M. Tet. Smooth medium purple with lovely form. Great daylily.

'**Child Bride**' Dor. 28" E. Tet. Re. Absolutely prolific butter yellow flowers in abundance. Strong growth, quick increase. (Plate 4)

'**Chinese Autumn**' Ev. 30" M. Re. Tet. Heavily pleated and ruffled flowers are a blend of coral, orange, rose, gold and apricot all aglow with irridescence. Superb in every way. (Plate 18)

'**Chinese Pavilion**' Ev. 30" E. M. Re. Tet. Large heavily textured pastel blend of cream, pink and rose. Very good.

'**Chinese Temple Flower**' Ev. E. M. 24" Re. Tet. Lilac lavender, bold purple band around triangular cream throat.

'**Chittagong**' Ev. 30" E. M. Re. Tet. Blend of peach, wine and rose with a yellow halo and throat. Continuous bloom.

'**Christmas Day**' Dor. 36" E. M. Re. Tet. Superior blood red with darker eye zone. Quality flowers on excellent scapes. (Cover)

'**Chrome Lemon**' Ev. 30" E. M. Large lemon yellow with diamond dusted petals. Lovely form and excellent growth.

'**Cinnamon Roll**' Dor. 30" M. Tet. Bright butter yellow. All dusted and brushed with cinnamon red. (Plate 10)

'**Commandment**' Dor. 30" M. Tet. Large bright pink orange blend giving a melon effect. Good growth. (Plate 48)

'**Coral Gem**' Ev. 32" E. M. Tet. Re. Super ruffled coral pink flowers with an orange throat. Great grower and continuous bloomer. Later scapes are up to 48" for us.

'**Cordon Rouge**' Ev. 26" Tet. Rounded ruffled rose pink self that grows well. (Plate 27)

Cosmic Hummingbird' Ev. 26" Dip. Re. Striking honey peach with a ruby red eye zone.

'**Court Noble**' Ev. 32" Well formed pastel coral, peach and rose blend with a yellow peach throat. Good grower.

'**Damascene**' Ev. 32" Re. Tet. Ruffled pastel lavender mauve with a lighter silver blue eye and ivory cream throat and green heart.

'Dancer' S.Ev. 18" E. M. Dip. Re. Soft pink with a dark red wine eye zone and green throat. (Plate 25)

'Dancing Shiva' S.Ev. 22" E. Tet. Re. Pefectly circular clear blue pink with overlapping heavily ruffled petals. One of the best. (Plate 24)

'Darius' Dor. 22" M. Tet. Purple with a darker eye zone. Good.

'Daydreamer' Ev. 26" M. Tet. Superior large flowers are blended apricot and cream. Top quality.

'Deborah Louise Ritchey' S.Ev. 16" E. M. Dip. Re. Light cream with a vibrant lavender eye zone.

'Delicate Treasure' S.Ev. 28" E. M. Tet. Re. Soft creamy pink blend. Wide ruffled petals.

'Disraeli' S.Ev. 28" E. M. Tet. Quality burgundy rose with a chalk white eye zone.

'Distant Chimes' Dor. 32" M. Tet. Large cream flowers with an ivory lemon overlay and green throat.

'Distant Glow' Dor. 28" Tet. Super glowing tangerine melon of outstanding form.

'Doll House' Dor. 27" E. M. Dip. Vibrant tangerine with pinkish lavender midribs and green heart. Heavily ruffled. Top quality. (Plate 31)

'Dorethe Louise' Dor. 28" E. M. Re. Tet. Super large green yellow ruffled flowers with a green throat. Excellent growth, continuous bloom, top quality. (Plate 93)

'Double Jackpot' Dor. 24" M. Tet. Clear light yellow double with a small green throat.

'Double Talk' S.Ev. 36" M. L. Re. Dip. Clear golden yellow double. Grows well. (Plate 51)

'Douglas Dale' Dor. 24" M. L. Tet. Re. Ruffled dusky red with a rich green throat. (Plate 14)

'Dress Circle' Dor. 24" M. Tet. Very round apricot orange with a rose pink flush. (Plate 28)

'Elizabeth Ann Hudson' Ev. 22" E. M. Tet. Re. Large flowered peach pink boldly edged and eyed purple. Grows well and rebloom is taller for us. (Plate 7)

'El Tigre' Ev. 30" E. M. Tet. Re. Large rounded bright tangerine with an olive green throat and darker eye zone. Very good. (Plate 26)

'Embassy' Ev. 30" E. M. L. Tet. Re. Round and ruffled rich plum burgundy. (Plate 11)

'Erin Prairie' Dor. 27" E. M. L. Tet. Green gold with grass green throat. Well formed.

'Etched in Gold' Dor. 20" E. M. Tet. Re. Primrose and pink blend with a frilly gold edge. (Plate 54)

'Eternal Blessing' Dor. 15" E. M. Dip. Re. Palest lemon, very close to white with pale throat. Blooms very well. (Plate 59)

'Ethiopia' Ev. 30" M. L. Tet. Re. Rich red purple flowers are round, full and overlapping.

'Eurasia' Ev. 28" E. M. Tet. Re. Flat ivory cream with rounded form and a pink glow.

'Fair Play' Dor. 27" Tet. Large vibrant light wine purple with a distinct ivory gold margin.

'Fannie Stadler' S.Ev. 30" M. L. Dip. Very bright rich red with a green throat.

'Favorite Things' Dor. 35" M. Dip. Rounded ruffled vibrant lemon yellow with a green heart.

'Feathered Friend' Dor. 28" M. Tet. Ruffled light brown with a mahogany eye zone. (Plate 41)

'Flames of Fortune' Dor. 30" E. M. Tet. Re. Variable colour from ivory cream to deep melon with a flamingo pink throat and irridescent glow. A really outstanding daylily. (Plate 95)

'Flaming Pearl' Dor. E. M. 24" Tet. Satin finished deep coral rose with orchid and pink highlights.

'Florence Byrd' Dor. M. 25" Tet. Large broad flat light yellow with a green throat.

'Florentine Prince' Dor. E. M. 32" Tet. Re. Burgundy wine with a lighter eye zone and small green throat.

'Folklorico' Dor. E. M. 33" Dip. Striking sunflower yellow overlaid with red and deeper eye zone. (Plate 34)

'Fondly Yours' Dor. E. M. 27" Tet. Pure glowing lemon yellow with a green throat.

'French Porcelain' Ev. 24" M. Tet. Smoky lavender mother of pearl with a bold plum wine eye zone. Broad overlapping petals are touched with gold edges.

'Full Welcome' Dor. 19" M. L. Tet. Low growing but large flowered clear light yellow.

'Galena Moon' Dor. 30" M. L. Tet. Round and full lemon yellow blend with a white midrib.

'Gallant Eyes' S.Ev. E. M. 27" Rose, striking purple eye zone and yellow green throat. (Plate 83)

'Garden Goddess' S.Ev. 28" Re. Tet. Large ivory cream flowers. Thick wax substance, ruffled flowers.

'Gauguin' Ev. 32" E. M. L. Tet. Re. Blend of coral, rose, tangerine and apricot. Excellent in every respect.

'Gay Cravat' Dor. 27" M. Tet. Light creamy pink with a large burgundy eye zone.

'Gentle Hearts' Dor. 30" M. L. Tet. Showy lavender orchid with green yellow heart.

'Ginger Jar' Ev. 28" E. M. Tet. Re. Amber tan to ginger brown, yellow throat. Very good. (Plate 89)

'Gleeman Song' Dor. 20" M. Tet. Ruffled light lemon with wide overlapping petals.

'Golden Milestone' Dor. 26" M. Tet. Flat golden yellow with round ruffled form. (Plate 43)

'Golden Prize' Dor. 26" M. Tet. Large ruffled and crepe textured golden yellow.

'Golden Surrey' Dor. 30" M. L. Tet. Clear golden yellow with fringed edges.

'Goya' Ev. 28" E. M. L. Tet. Re. Peach pink with delicate pink highlights.

'Grand Opera' S.Ev. 30" E. M. Tet. Re. Cherry to rose red. Flat, round, ruffled and spectacular.

'Grape Harvest' Dor. 27" M. Tet. Large rosy purple with a deep purple eye and light yellow throat.

'Grape Velvet' Dor. 24" E. M. Dip. Re. Lovely dark purple with a small lime heart. Ruffled overlapping petals. A favourite. (Plate 46)

'Green Dragon' S.Ev. 34" E. M. Dip. Re. Greenish yellow with a green throat. (Plate 57)

'Green Fringe' S.Ev. 27" M. Tet. Very green effect from this green yellow. Lovely fringed petals.

'Green Glade' Dor. 30" M. Tet. Full round ruffled pale coral pink, deep apple green throat. (Plate 63)

'Heather Green' Dor. 30" M. L. Tet. Re. Beautiful pink blend with a green throat. (Plate 47)

'Helen Boehm' Dor. 32" M. L. Tet. Large porcelain cream brushed lavender.

'Hey There' Dor. 28" M. Tet. Crimson red with a smooth velvet finish. Wide, ruffled petals.

'Hidden Dream' Dor. 28" M. L. Tet. Heavily ruffled and fluted pink blend with amber edges.

'Higashi' Ev. 24" E. M. Tet. Re. Broad porcelain smooth ivory, flesh pink. (Plate 100)

'Highland Lass' S.Ev. 30" M. Tet. Re. Large bicolour with strawberry pink petals and cream sepals brushed light pink. (Plate 40)

'High Priestess' Ev. 42" M.L. Tet. Tall pastel bicolour of pink and creamy yellow.

'Hope Diamond' Dor. 14" E. M. Dip. Re. Lovely light cream with diamond dusting, ruffling and crimping. Top quality. (Plate 36)

'Hudson Valley' S.Ev. 32" M. Tet. Huge green yellow with a green throat. Flowers over 8" in diameter.

'Ida Wimberly Munson' Ev. 26" M. L. Tet. Large lilac pink of super quality. (Plate 44)

'Imperial Damask' Dor. 26" M. Tet. Multi blend of flesh pink, peach coral, gold and rose.

'Imperial Watermark' Ev. 30" M. L. Tet. Re. Rosy wine with an ivory rose watermark.

'Inca Torch' Dor. 21" M. L. Tet. Re. Bright tangerine orange with rounded petals. Heavy texture.

'Indonesia' Dor. 24" M. Tet. Large full and flat yellow of superb quality. (Plate 42)

'Ivory Marble' Ev. 30" E. M. Tet. Re. Rich ivory flowers with a crisp marble like texture.

'Jamaican Drum' Dor. 32" M. Tet. Large orange pink blend with gold amber edges and a deep olive throat.

'James Marsh' Dor. 24" M. Tet. What a flower! Bright scarlet with deeper hues and yellow green throat. Heavily ruffled and super round form. The best red yet. (Plate 1)

'Jane Austen' Dor. 34" M. Tet. Wide deep rose pink with a deeper halo and soft yellow throat. Stylish. (Plate 91)

'Japanese Royal' Ev. 30" M. L. Tet. Well formed rich grape purple with a lemon throat.

'June Melody' Dor. 30" M. Tet. Re. Clear bright medium pink.

'June Wine' Dor. 28" M. Tet. Re. Lavender pink with purple edges, purple halo and green throat. Great.

'Just Dorothy' S.Ev. 24" E. M. Dip. Straw yellow with a wide burgundy eye zone.

'Kannon' Ev. 28" M. Tet. Triangular formed pastel blend of peach and pink with an ivory throat.

'Kara Kum' Ev. 28" E. M. Tet. Re. Large blended cream and pink with a lime green throat.

'Kempion' Dor. 34" M. Tet. Re. Light creamy pink with a wide lavender halo and green throat. Very worthwhile and popular daylily.

'Kings Cloak' Ev. 25" E. M. Tet. Re. Large soft rosy pink with a magenta influence. Heavy bloomer.

'Kistabel' Ev. 16" M. L. Tet. Re. Ruffled and beautiful blended light coral pink of large size on a low plant. One of the best pinks.

'**Knave**' Ev. 25" M. L. Tet. Re. Deep rosy wine with a precise cream throat.

'**La Charmante**' Ev. 24" M. L. Tet. Re. Large ruffled rose pink with a very large cream yellow throat. Good quality.

'**La Peche**' Ev. 24" M. L. Tet. Re. Beautiful frilly, ruffled rich apricot peach self. Excellent daylily. (Plate 79)

'**La Scala**' Ev. 30" M. Tet. Deep blend of rose, red and cerise with a rosy eye zone.

'**Lemon Grass**' S.Ev. 22" M. Tet. Ruffled and rounded lemon yellow of excellent form. Some rebloom for us.

'**Lions Pride**' Dor. 28" M. Tet. Re. Large buff flowers brushed copper. Very heavy bloomer.

'**Lippizaner**' Dor. 32" E. M. Dip. A very light cream, nearly white with a green throat. Large ruffled flowers. Has rebloomed for us.

'**Little Fat Dazzler**' S.Ev. 26" Dip. Min. Re. Small ruffled prolific rose red.

'**Little Grapette**' S.Ev. 12" E. Dip. Min. An outstanding miniature with 2" flowers, round and ruffled grape purple.

'**Little Green Apples**' Ev. E. M. Re. Min. My favourite miniature. Rounded 3" flowers of blended green yellow with a green throat. Heavy bloom and superb daylily. (Plate 5)

'**Loch Leman**' Dor. 33" M. Tet. Rose lavender with a large magenta eye zone.

'**Loisteen Kirkman**' Dor. M. 27" Tet. Large flowers of an unusual blue purple colour.

'**Look Once Again**' Dor. 30" M. Tet. Re. Very heavily ruffled light cantaloupe orange with rounded form and diamond dusting.

'**Lord Camden**' Dor. M. 24" Dip. Small flowered rounded and well formed red with a small green throat. (Plate 23)

'**Lorraine Kilgore**' S.Ev. M. 30" Re. Tet. Electric coral pink self. Apricot throat. Super.

'**Loyal Subject**' Dor. 26" M. Tet. Re. Pastel apricot and cream blend.

'**Lullaby Baby**' Ev. 18" Dip. Heavily ruffled 3½" super pastel pink.

'**Luna Danca**' Dor. 14" E. M. Dip. Re. Very close to white. Medium sized soft cream flowers in profusion.

'**Magic Kiss**' Ev. 26" M. Tet. Re. Outstanding pastel pink with a darker eye zone. Large flowered and profuse bloom.

'**Magnifique**' Ev. 30" E. M. L. Tet. Re. Subtle blend of yellow, cream, ivory, flesh and pink. Lime green throat.

'**Malaysian Spice**' Ev. 22" E. M. Tet. Re. Large rounded blend of rose, peach, pink and amber. (Plate 38)

'**Malihini**' Dor. 26" M. Tet. Heavily ruffled yellow with a faint rose brushing. Crinkled edges. Super.

'**Manchurian Apricot**' Ev. E. M. 22" Tet. Re. 6" flowers of warm pale apricot shaded flesh pink. Gold edge.

'**Mandarin's Coat**' Ev. 25" E. M. Tet. Re. Wine red with a patterned damask eye.

'**Mary Helen**' Ev. E. M. 30" Dip. Re. Wide ruffled honey yellow blend.

'**Mary Todd**' Dor. 26" E. M. L. Tet. Re. All time favourite ruffled 6" blooms of clear bright yellow. (Plate 37)

'**Mask Ball**' Ev. 32" E. M. Tet. Rounded flowers are soft pastel yellow and peach with a bold wine purple eye zone. (Plate 50)

'**May Unger**' Ev. 22" E. M. Tet. Re. Rose pink with a green throat and rounded form.

'**Meadow Mystic**' Dor. 23" M. Tet. Re. Good dark lavender with a green throat. (Plate 80)

'**Mercy Me**' Dor. 30" E. M. Dip. Re. Nice light purple with creamy midribs and yellow green heart.

'**Mild Manner**' Dor. 29" M. Tet. Re. Ruffled and recurved creamy yellow with pink midribs.

'**Ming Treasure**' Ev. 20" E. M. Tet. Re. Bold coral rose of rounded form, fluted and ruffled. Green gold throat. (Plate 35)

'**Mironique**' Dor. 24" M. Tet. Re. Coral and lemon blend with a pale blue pink line on the petals. Triangular form.

'**Mountain Violet**' Ev. 28" M. Tet. Re. Rich violet purple with recurved petals. Outstanding for growth, flower production and colour.

'**Music of Love**' Ev. 34" E. M. L. Tet. Re. Blend of pink, salmon and coral. Lemon throat and gold edge. Lovely. (Plate 8)

'**My Belle**' Ev. E. 30" Dip. Re. 6" Pastel pink flowers with green throat. Great!

'**My Rosary**' Ev. 34" E. M. Dip. Re. How do you describe this super daylily without too many superlatives? Creamy buff flowers with a green throat outpouring on to the petals are produced in absolute profusion. Flowers are ruffled and wide, produced throughout the season on scapes that carry from 60 to over 100 flowers each. Fantastic! (Plate 72)

'My Ways' Dor. 36" E. M. Dip. Re. Ruffled velvet red with green throat. Petals overlap and slightly recurve. Excellent growe (Plate 9)

'Naomi Ruth' Dor. 30" E. M. Min. Lovely miniature with rounded ruffled apricot pink flowers in profusion. (Plate 3)

'Nuka' S.Ev. 28" E. M. Tet. Re. Large rounded copper pink flower with a copper halo and green throat.

'Oh Perfect Love' Ev. 26" E. Dip. Re. Cream with a light lavender eye zone and green throat.

'Olive Bailey Langdon' Ev. 28" E. Tet. Re. Rich deep violet purple flowers are rounded, overlapping and ruffled. Almost continually in bloom through the season. A favourite. (Plate 32)

'Orange Parade' Dor. 30" E. M. Dip. Pale orange to apricot with a glowing heart.

'Orange Prelude' Dor. 28" E. Tet. Re. Brilliant golden orange of outstanding garden qualities.

'Orange Slice' S.Ev. 30" E. M. Tet. Light but bright orange with dark yellow midribs and edges.

'Pagoda Goddess' Ev. M. 30" Tet. Re. Shimmering pastel of lime, cream and pink.

'Palace Guard' Ev. 28" M. L. Tet. Re. Chinese red with a satin sheen and full and overlapping petals.

'Paper Lanterns' Ev. 24" Tet. Re. Creamy lemon with heavy ruffling and crepe texture. Absolutely superb. (Plate 82)

'Pass Me Not' Ev. 24" E. M. L. Dip. Re. Ruffled, rounded and crimped petals of creamy orange yellow with a bright maroon eye and green heart. One of the best. (Plate 66)

'Pearl Island' Dor. 28" M. Tet. Ruffled and flat white to pale pink with satin texture.

'Peekaboo Eyes' E. 18" Dip. Re. 6" Light yellow, purple eye zone, green throat.

'Persian Market' Ev. 27" M. Tet. Re. Large deep rose pink with a rose red eye zone.

'Phoenecian Pearls' Ev. 30" M. Tet. Re. Pale orchid pink with a violet blue eye zone.

'Pink Pleasure' Ev. 20" E. Dip. Re. Powder pink of medium size and prolific bloom.

'Poets Rhyme' Ev. 24" M. Tet. Re. Flat and broad ruffled pink blend.

'Quannah' S.Ev. 30" M. Tet. Re. Bright copper orange with a small yellow green throat.

'Quinn Buck' S.Ev. 26" M. Tet. Heavily ruffled and well formed blue lavender with a faint halo of deeper lavender. Super. (Plate 70)

'Rahotep' S.Ev. 28" M. L. Tet. Re. Very round rose red of fine form and growth.

'Rainbow Skies' Ev. 36" E. M. Tet. Re. Lovely citrus lemon with pink highlights and lime throat.

'Rare Gift' Ev. 30" E. M. Tet. Re. Smoky rose blended ashes of roses with a silvery blue eye and cream throat. Lovely form and unique colour.

'Real Wind' Dor. 28" M. L. Tet. Re. Pink orange with a wide rose eye zone, ruffled edges and recurved blooms. Different and pleasing. (Plate 62)

'Regal Tapestry' Ev. 30" M. Tet. Re. Large, broad flat and ruffled creamy gold with wide burgundy purple chevrons. Outstanding. (Plate 92)

'Renaissance Fair' Ev. 28" E. M. Tet. Re. Silvery mauve with a dark purple burgundy eye zone. Broad, flat and triangular form. Heavy bloomer. (Plate 81)

'Robes of Psyche' Ev. 24" E. M. Dip. Re. Medium pink and ivory blend giving a self effect. Broad recurved petals.

'Round Table' Dor. 32" M. Tet. Re. Strawberry pink with pale pink veining. Heavily fringed and ruffled flowers of superior form. (Plate 6)

'Royal Diamond' Ev. 30" M. Tet. Re. Nice blend of copper and brown tones. Good grower.

'Royal Heritage' Ev. 36" E. M. L. Tet. Re. Rich violet lavender flowers are large, broad, flat and slightly recurved. Top quality.

'Royal Kin' Dor. 29" M. Tet. Broad, ruffled and crimped yellow flowers with a cream margin.

'Ruffled Apricot' Dor. 28" E. M. Tet. Large intense glowing apricot flowers are heavily ruffled and beautifully formed.

'Ruffled Magic' S.Ev. E. M. 25" Tet. Clear yellow, pink undertones, small green throat.

'Russian Rhapsody' Ev. 30" M. Tet. Re. Spectacular ruffled plum purple with bold purple eye zone. Heavy substance and top quality. Good rebloom. (Plate 65)

'Ruwenzori' Ev. 30" E. M. L. Tet. Re. Ruffled lavender mauve with vibrant purple eye and overlapping petals. Heavy bloomer.

'Sacred Shield' Dor. 24" M. Tet. Very round vibrant tangerine pink.

'Samurai Silk' Ev. 28" M. Tet. Re. Wide bright orange, coral with a bold yellow coral eye. Large flowers.

'Sari' Ev. 20" M. Dip. Re. Lovely round overlapping and ruffled petals of pink with rose highlights. Outstanding quality. There is an induced tetraploid 'Sari' available now.

'Satin Silk' Dor. 32" M. Tet. Re. Smooth pink blend with a green throat. Well formed large flowers.

'Scaramouche' Ev. 28" M. Tet. Very popular and unusual silvery mauve with a boldly patterned burgundy eye zone.

'Scarlet Gem' Ev. 30" M. L. Tet. Re. Round petalled ruffled red of excellent growth and form.

'Scarlock' Dor. 30" M. Tet. Super round petalled clear red with a green throat. One of the best. (Plate 96)

'Scotsboro' Dor. 26" M. Tet. Clear light lavender with a narrow wine circle and lemon throat.

'Scottish Belle' Dor. 20" M. Tet. Ruffled rose pink blend with a yellow throat.

'Sea of Stars' Dor. 36" M. L. Tet. Impressive lavender blend with a green throat. Soft colours and pretty.

'Secret Garden' Ev. 30" M. Tet. Large circular flowers are deep peach pink with a rose orchid halo.

'Seductress' Ev. E. M. 18" Dip. Super beige lavender edged with purple. Purple halo. (Plate 61)

'Sensuous Summer' Dor. 32" M. Tet. Re. Ruffled peach pink with an apricot throat.

'Shamrock Rose' Dor. 40" M. L. Tet. Re. Lipstick pink with an apple green throat. Reblooms for us.

'Short Stuff' Ev. 16" E. M. Tet. Re. Dawn pink with a rose pink halo and chartreuse throat. Masses of well formed flowers.

'Siloam Bo Peep' Dor. E. M. 18" Min. Orchid pink with vivid purple eye.

'Siloam Fairy Tale' Dor. E. M. 18" Min. 2½" flowers of frosted creamy pink and orchid eye. (Plate 56)

'Silver Veil' Ev. 24" E. M. Tet. Re. Bluish silvery lavender with a precisely patterned yellow throat. Different and very nice.

'Simply Pretty' Dor. M. L. 26" Tet. Re. Deep persimmon self with a green throat. Heavily ruffled flowers are produced in profusion. Super daylily. (Plate 86)

'Sir Oliver' Ev. 20" E. M. Tet. Pastel magenta violet with lighter pink eye. (Plate 60)

'So Lovely' S.Ev. 30" M. Dip. Re. Very pale cream, near white, green throat. So lovely and oh so popular.

'South Rim' Ev. 36" M. L. Dip. Re. Vigorous butter yellow with a wide red eye zone and triangular form.

'Spanish Brocade' Dor. 22" M. Dip. Cardinal red with gold edging and orange throat. Ruffled flowers, good form and some rebloom for us.

'Tammas' Dor. 29" M. L. Tet. Large raspberry purple with a green yellow throat.

'Teahouse Tapestry' Ev. 22" E. M. Tet. Re. Soft silver lilac with a pale mauve sheen and rose plum eye zone.

'Terra' S.Ev. 29" M. Tet. Re. Super rich deep melon that absolutely glows. Very large flowers.

'Thai Ballet' Dor. 28" M. Tet. Re. Vibrant rich magenta rose orchid edged purple.

'Tiffany Gold' Ev. 24" E. M. Dip. Re. 7" flowers in yellow with crepe texture.

'Tiffany Palace' Ev. 28" E. M. Dip. Re. Pastel ivory pink and smoky mauve with a large cream patterned throat.

'Touched By Midas' Ev. 30" E. M. Tet. Very bright rich gold self. Lovely form. An outstanding daylily.

'Tovarich' Ev. 30" E. M. L. Tet. Re. Vigorous and prolific dark red black. Just about the best in the very dark shades. (Plate 85)

'Tranquil Aura' Dor. 36" E. M. Tet. Re. Pure green gold diamond dusted, ruffled and crimped.

'Twenty Third Psalm' Ev. 28" E. M. Dip. Re. Ruffled clear pale pink with a darker halo and chartreuse throat.

'Twilight Crepe' Ev. 20" E. M. Dip. Re. Peach and pink blend all creped and ruffled.

'Twilight Swan' Ev. 28" Tet. Re. 5" Pastel flesh pink with a cream throat.

'Valedictorian' Ev. 30" M. L. Tet. Re. Excellent tangerine rose blend with a lighter eye zone. (Plate 71)

'Vatican Knight' Ev. 28" E. M. Tet. Re. Pale mauve with a dark rose eye zone and cream throat. Vigorous and prolific.

'Veiled Magic' Ev. 24" M. Tet. Re. Soft pastel cream with a lemon throat. (Plate 69)

'Veiled Organdy' Dor. 30" M. Tet. Re. Lemon, overlaid pink, apricot and chartreuse. Ruffled flowers.

'**Venetian Magistrate**' Ev. 24" E. M. Tet. Re. Spectacular triangular flowers are violet mauve with strong geometric cream pattern around throat. (Plate 64)

'**Venetian Splendor**' Ev. 18" E. M. Tet. Re. Yellow petals and rosy mauve sepals. Reverse bicolour with electric plum purple eye zone and purple edging. Unique.

'**Viracocha**' Dor. 25" M. Tet. Large brilliant tangerine with heavy crepe substance and outstanding quality.

'**Vizcaya**' Ev. 29" M. Tet. Re. Large broad flesh pink to cream of good form.

'**Wally Nance III**' Dor. 25" E. M. Dip. Re. Bright ruby red with a green heart. Ruffled overlapping petals.

'**Waterbird**' Ev. 32" M. Tet. Ruffled pastel blend of lavender, violet and cream. Pretty and popular.

'**Wine Bold**' Dor. 29" M. Tet. Wine purple with a yellow green throat. Nice form.

'**Yasmin**' Ev. 30" E. M. Tet. Re. Super pastel in cream, yellow and pink. Ruffled and nicely formed. (Plate 73)

'**Yellow Kitten**' Dor. 17" E. M. Dip. 5" Greenish lemon yellow with heavy ruffles.

'**Your Song**' Ev. 42" E. M. Tet. Re. Very tall, vigorous and large flowered rose pink with an intense darker eye zone.

'**Zambia**' Dor. 30" M. Tet. Dark black red with a star shaped green throat.

Sources of Supply

New South Wales	Rainbow Ridge Nursery (Graeme and Helen Grosvenor and John Taylor) 8 Taylors Rd, Dural 2158 (also Iris)
Victoria	Tempo Two Nursery (Barry and Lesley Blyth) 57-59 East Rd, Pearcedale 3912 (also Iris)
Queensland	Daylily Display Centre (M. Flanders and M. Mead) Tirroan, Gin Gin 4671
	Mountain View Daylily Nursery (Scott Alexander) McCarthy's Rd, Maleny 4552
	K. Simpson 39 Amega St, Mt Gravatt 4122
	Wyamba Gardens (Mr & Mrs J. Agnew) 33 Woodford Rd, Pullenvale 4069
Tasmania	Woolnorth Station (K. & L. Else) Montagu Via Smithton 7330

7. PHOTOGRAPHING DAYLILIES

If you have a collection of daylilies it is a pleasant extension of your hobby to photograph them and be able to enjoy them throughout the year. Best results will be obtained by using good equipment such as a single lens reflex camera with a macro lens.

Daylily photographs can be taken as portraits of single blooms, scapes carrying a number of open blooms, clumps with many blooms in evidence or general landscaping photographs.

Photographing daylilies is a fascinating adventure as the flower can vary so much in its single day of life both in terms of colour and form and flowers vary considerably from day to day. Indeed one could obtain a collection of photographs of any one particular daylily. There is no particular time of day which is best suited for daylily photography and most flowers will give absolutely beautiful photographs.

Best results for single bloom photography are obtained by looking into the flower with interesting variations being obtained by taking part side on photographs. For a true portrait giving all details of throat and heart variation of colour, it is essential however to look into the flower and use a reflector to ensure good lighting right into the heart. This reflector can be made by stretching aluminium foil over a base and directing sunlight to cover the whole bloom. Care should be taken to ensure that sufficient depth of field is allowed to have clarity of the petal outline, the heart of the flower and the stamens and stigma, all of which are in different planes. I would recommend the use of 64 A.S.A. colour film and aperture selection of f 8 or f 11 to ensure this overall clarity.

Daylily scapes are often not easy to photograph as the flowers are invariably facing in different directions, making it difficult to compose your photo. This can be remedied by removing clean fresh flowers and positioning them in the branches to obtain the optimum effect. All dead flowers should be removed and care should be taken to ensure that the foliage is clean and the background is pleasant or suitably thrown out of focus by selecting an aperture in the f 4 or f 5.6 range.

To obtain a satisfactory photograph of a daylily clump it is essential to groom the whole clump with particular attention to day old flowers which look quite messy. Those spent flowers usually fall and self groom the clump after the second day. Any finished scapes should be carefully cut away and removed as these will look most unsightly. If there are unfilled gaps in the clump these can be filled by cutting individual flowers and repositioning them in the desired position or cutting whole spikes and repositioning them by boring holes in the ground and inserting them.

For landscape photographs individual attention to the grooming of plants is less critical, but care must be taken to frame the photograph and present an interesting overall effect.

Remember that it is far better to take all the above care and be pleased with your results than to be slapdash and obtain unsatisfactory results. I suggest you use the word fast to ensure satisfactory results:

F for FOCUS — a clear sharp subject with an unobtrusive background

A for APERTURE — try to work at f 8, f 11 or f 16 for best results and use a reflector to obtain even lighting

S for SPEED — try to work at 1/60 sec or faster, otherwise use a tripod

T for THINK — think about the framing of the subject, the foreground, the background, the grooming of the daylilies and the positioning of the camera

HYBRIDISING

In hybridising, a large number of seedlings from any one cross should be raised to explore the potential of the cross. Hybridisers fall into three categories — those who just collect seed and plant it out with high hopes; those who dab a bit of pollen here and there, again with a lot of hope but little care and planning; and those scientific breeders who examine family trees, plan crosses, set great quantities of pods and thoroughly test the full potential of any planned cross. While there is a place for all three in breeding hemerocallis, there is little doubt that the scientific breeder will have the greatest chance of success.

As is the case with any other type of plant, the hemerocallis hybridiser is primarily concerned with form and colour. Even the most rank novice will be amazed and delighted with the variation in form and colour that can be obtained from one cross. It seems that there is endless variety, and this alone should give a great deal of pleasure to the amateur grower.

Before a seedling is registered and named, however, there are other significant considerations. These factors are growth, scapes, number of buds, amount of rebloom, health and vigour. The most important question is whether the seedling is a new colour or pattern or an improvement on all others available in the same colour or pattern. It is only when one gets a positive response to all of these considerations that thought should

be given to naming, registering and possibly introducing a daylily.

The registration of daylilies is done through the American Hemerocallis Society whose registrar issues the necessary registration data sheets, which must be completed in triplicate. Two sheets are returned to the A.H.S. and one is retained by the hybridiser. The current registrar (1986) is W.E. Monroe, 2244 Cloverdale Av., Baton Rouge, La 70808 U.S.A. Basic descriptive data required is

(1) Proposed Name (and alternatives)

(2) Height of scape in inches

(3) Season of bloom: Extra Early, Early, Early Midseason, Midseason, Late Midseason, Late, Very Late, Reblooming or Remontant

(4) Colour and pattern

(5) Foliage habit

(6) Other desirable information including bloom habit, i.e. diurnal, nocturnal or extended, fragrance, parentage and seedling number.

No names can be reserved and applications and requests for names will be considered by the registrar only when made on formal applications for registration and accompanied by fees. Registrations from countries other than the U.S.A. and Canada are accepted without fee.

The name of the hybrid should be registered by the originator unless a selector has acquired stock prior to registration, when it may be registered by the selector. No limit is placed on the number of daylilies which one may register in any one year but breeders are urged to exercise the greatest restraint in the selection of hybrids for naming.

The checklist of hemerocallis species and hybrids registered from 1893 to 1957 fills some 218 pages of a book and runs to over 7000 cultivars. Registrations in recent years run to somewhere around 800 per year, so it would seem that about 30 000 different cultivars have been named and registered. Of course many of these would no longer be available and many would not have crossed the equator into the southern hemisphere.

So much for the philosophy behind making a cross and following it up with the subsequent naming and registration of the progeny, but what of the mechanics of making the cross. The procedure is relatively simple. Once the parents have been selected, take the anther of the daylily to be used as pollen parent and rub the pollen across the stigma of the intended pod parent. Record the cross on a tag and label the pollinated flower.

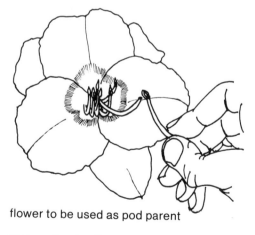

obtain pollen from selected pollen parent

flower to be used as pod parent

apply pollen to stigma

Hybridising daylilies

The pod parent is always written first. Thus if pollen from 'Chinese Autumn' is to be put onto a flower of 'Ginger Jar', the cross is recorded as 'Ginger Jar' x 'Chinese Autumn'. Flowers do not have to be covered or handled in any special way once the cross is made. The best time to make a cross for maximum seed setting is early in the morning on cool days. The later in the day that pollination is left and the warmer the day the less likely the probability of a 'take'.

There are some cultivars which are infertile one way or another. Some will not set seed under any circumstances while others do not have viable pollen. One must be very careful to cross only diploids with diploids or tetraploids with tetraploids, as diploids will not cross with tetraploids.

If your cross has 'taken', and you have roughly one chance in three of this happening if you have observed all the above, you will notice a swelling of the ovary at the base of the old flower in about 3-4 days. In anything from 60-80 days the pod will be mature and ready for collection. As they approach maturity the pods, which would normally be the size of a large marble, turn brown, begin to dry and start to crack open at the top. At this stage they should be checked daily and harvested as soon as they start to crack. Once harvested, the seeds should be stored in envelopes or open containers until ready for planting. Planting time differs according to climate; in tropical northern areas seed can be planted immediately, while in colder areas it may be kept stored until the following spring. Any seeds held over past autumn should be kept in a refrigerator to ensure maximum germination. Some hybridisers soak the seed for 24 hours before planting, while others insert a small nick in the outer casing of the seed prior to sowing. There are claims that this increases the percentage of germination.

Seeds are best sown in a seed raising mix

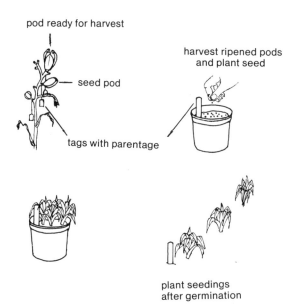

pod ready for harvest

seed pod

tags with parentage

harvest ripened pods
and plant seed

plant seedings
after germination

Seedlings

either in pots, cold frames or straight into garden rows, and you will have to learn for yourself the best and most appropriate methods.

Germination can be erratic and your climatic conditions will determine whether you see your precious seedlings in just a few days or have to wait weeks. Raising the seedlings is not difficult and will depend on initial sowing conditions, but pot sown plants can be set out within two months of germination if climatic conditions allow.

Most hybridisers start out a little erratically using those flowers that are out at the time. Once you develop to the planned cross stage and wish to make crosses that are not possible because the flowers are not out simultaneously, you will need to hold pollen over a period of time. Pollen can be collected and will remain viable for days and even weeks if kept cold and dry. Once collected, the pollen should be scraped into an empty gelatin capsule, labelled and placed in a small plastic container into which has been placed some silica-gel and the whole lot kept in a refrigerator. When ready for use remove the pollen, allow it to warm to room temperature (this will be relatively quick) and then proceed with the cross.

As well as keeping your record of any crosses made dangling from the pollinated flower, it is a good idea to keep a book, recording crosses made, date, time of day and all relevant information. Tags do become untied, eaten, wet and the separate recording of information is essential. Also complete records will help the hybridiser to learn all the facets which go to make a successful hybridising venture. It is one thing to read about it, but by far the best teacher is the accumulated knowledge obtained by actually doing the job. You will learn the do's and don'ts and you will learn what information is of value and what is not.

Once involved in a hybridising campaign, it is very desirable to have goals and work towards these. In evaluating your own seedlings you need to be ruthless and accept only those which are distinct from cultivars already named and improvements on these cultivars. When it comes to a question of naming and registering or not the best advice is: if in doubt, DON'T! At least seek the opinion of a knowledgeable associate who is not afraid to give an honest opinion. Hybridisers should not be 'thin skinned' and perhaps should not even ask an opinion unless they are reasonably sure that they have a winner. Remember also that cultivars will not always perform well everywhere and it is often a good idea to have new cultivars spread around a little for evaluation before they are named and registered.

Here are a few definitions, with apologies to the Oxford English Dictionary and further apologies to the writer of an article in an old American Hemerocallis Society bulletin from which I stole some of the ideas:

Avid Hybridiser Have you seen my things? They are so much better than . . .

Terrific My seedlings.

It doesn't take the sun *Your* seedling.

Dormant Lousy in the north.

Evergreen Lousy in the south.

Popularity Poll I don't want to vote for my own but what else is there?

Avid Hybridiser (again) The conditions are not right for it here. You should see it at home!

Registration I have a good name which isn't on the checklist. Now to find a plant to match it.

Colour Of course it wilts by noon, but . . .

Imagination It fades attractively.

Optimist I will have one good enough to name next year.

Substance Oh yes . . . but *I* am working on *colour*.

Objectivity I never knock other people's things but my stuff is good *everywhere*.

9. DAYLILIES FOR EATING

One of the major problems for any hybridiser is what to do with the many unwanted seedlings once a decision has been made as to what to keep. Not so with daylily hybridisers — those you don't like or don't want in the garden you just eat. This is also the solution for excess stock of certain cultivars or those antiquated cultivars ready to be replaced.

Daylilies have been used for centuries by the Chinese in their cooking and the daylily is an ideal vegetable in that all its parts are edible. The early daylily stalks can be cut just above the roots and the tender inner section can be boiled for a few minutes and eaten just as asparagus with butter. These stalks can also be sliced and added to salads.

The small tubers attached to the roots and having the appearance of mini potatoes are also usable. The older soft 'bulbs' should be discarded and the young, firm and crisp 'bulbs' can be enjoyed raw for a sweet, nutty flavour or can be used in salads, boiled or creamed. These young 'tubers' are white, as distinct from the older brown ones, and their taste has been variously described as resembling that of peas, nuts, radish or water chestnut. They can be cooked and used in Chinese dishes where they retain their crispness in the best Chinese tradition. Just what does a daylily taste like? As well as the above descriptions it has been described as being 'bean like', 'mushroom like' and 'asparagus like'. Probably the best answer is to try them for yourself and make your own evaluation.

The daylily flower can be collected for eating at any stage of blooming. It is generally accepted that the buds are at their best for eating when very full, so they are picked on the day before opening. They are an excellent substitute for green beans if boiled for four minutes and served with butter and salt. They can also be dipped in a thick egg batter and fried in hot fat. The open flower can be treated in exactly the same way, and there are those aesthetic gourmets who want the best of both worlds and so enjoy the flower and then use the spent blooms for cooking with no less desirable results.

The flavour of soups and stews is enhanced by using buds or flowers, which should be added during the last minutes that the dishes are simmered. If there is an excess of flowers for summer use, when stews and soups are not so popular in this country, they can be stored away. The blooms can be dried in a warm room, stored in glass jars and used in the winter months when these foods are popular.

Here are a few suggestions from the American Hemerocallis Society publication *Everything You've Always Wanted to Know About Daylilies*, reprinted with the society's permission.

Freezing Daylilies
Daylilies freeze as well as any other standard

garden vegetable and may be enjoyed throughout the year. The buds and spent blossoms are usually frozen because of ease of handling.

Daylilies of almost any colour can be used. It is said the red ones have a bitter taste. Preferable are the yellows, oranges, and pastels — even pale pinks are delicious.

When daylilies are dropped into hot water they have a tendency to open, so if you wish the buds to remain closed, pick them about two days before their normal time to open. To freeze, bring blanching kettle to a rolling boil. Drop in only enough daylilies to be covered. After the water returns to a boil, blanch for three minutes. Remove and chill in cold water. Drain well and pack in freezer bags.

Fried Daylilies

(non-scented varieties preferred)
Dip approximately one dozen fresh or thawed daylilies in beaten egg (one egg is usually sufficient to coat a dozen lilies). Roll in a mixture of flour, salt and onion powder. Sauté in hot oil until crisp.

Sautéed Daylilies

Put thawed or fresh daylilies in a non-stick skillet or shallow pan, salt, cover and let simmer until tender. *Do not overcook.* Be sure all moisture is used up. Remove from pan, add butter if desired, sprinkle well with onion powder. Serve while hot.

Daylily Bud Casserole

2 qts hemerocallis buds
3-4 strips of bacon
2 onions
1 can sliced mushrooms
1 can cream of mushroom soup
1 can water chestnuts

Cook bacon until crisp. Remove from pan and set aside. Brown onions slowly in bacon drippings. Add 1/2 to 3/4 cup water. When it reaches the boiling point, add hemerocallis buds. Season with salt and peper to taste. Cook until tender, being careful not to overcook. Add drained mushrooms and water chestnuts, sliced or whole. Slowly and gently fold in undiluted soup. Turn into a casserole dish, garnish top with crumbled bacon and bake in 350°F oven until bubbly.

INDEX

(Numbers in **bold** refer to Plates)